D0098895

LIVE

/ L I V / *verb*

remain alive, be alive at a specified time,

have an exciting or fulfilling life

SADIE ROBERTSON

WITH BETH CLARK

THOMAS NELSON
Since 1798

Published in Nashville, Tennessee, by Tommy Nelson. Tommy Nelson is an imprint of Thomas Nelson. Thomas Nelson is a registered trademark of HarperCollins Christian Publishing, Inc.

Published in association with William Morris Endeavor Entertainment, LLC, c/o Mel Berger and Margaret Riley King, 11 Madison Avenue, New York, New York 10010.

Tommy Nelson titles may be purchased in bulk for educational, business, fund-raising, or sales promotional use. For information, please e-mail SpecialMarkets@ThomasNelson.com.

Italics in Scripture indicate the author's emphasis.

All Scripture quotations, unless otherwise indicated, are taken from the Holy Bible, New International Version®, NIV®. Copyright © 1973, 1978, 1984, 2011 by Biblica, Inc.® Used by permission of Zondervan. All rights reserved worldwide. www.zondervan.com. The "NIV" and "New International Version" are trademarks registered in the United States Patent and Trademark Office by Biblica, Inc.®

Scripture quotations marked AMP are taken from the Amplified® Bible, Copyright © 2015 by The Lockman Foundation. Used by permission. www.lockman.org.

Scripture quotations marked MSG are taken from THE MESSAGE, copyright © 1993, 2002, 2018 by Eugene H. Peterson. Used by permission of NavPress. All rights reserved. Represented by Tyndale House Publishers, a Division of Tyndale House Ministries.

Scripture quotations marked NKJV are taken from the New King James Version®. © 1982 by Thomas Nelson. Used by permission. All rights reserved.

Scripture quotations marked NLT are taken from the Holy Bible, New Living Translation. © 1996, 2004, 2007, 2013, 2015 by Tyndale House Foundation. Used by permission of Tyndale House Publishers, Inc., Carol Stream, Illinois 60188. All rights reserved.

Scripture quotations marked TPT are from The Passion Translation®. Copyright © 2017, 2018 by Passion & Fire Ministries, Inc. Used by permission. All rights reserved. ThePassionTranslation.com.

ISBN 978-1-4002-1308-5 (audiobook)
ISBN 978-1-4002-1307-8 (eBook)

Library of Congress Cataloging-in-Publication Data is on file.
ISBN 978-1-4002-1306-1

Photography copyright © Jayda Rust.

Printed in the United States of America
20 21 22 23 24 PC/LSCC 6 5 4 3 2 1
Mfr: LSC / Crawfordsville, IN / January 2020 / PO #9559565

To those who struggle to celebrate life,

may these words lead you on a journey

to abundant and everlasting life.

Contents

Foreword

BY KORIE ROBERTSON

I'M ON A PLANE THINKING I SHOULD USE MY TIME WISELY TO write this foreword. However, there is a tiny television screen in front of me, and the flight attendant offered me headphones, and the truth is, I've been a little intimidated by this task. How do you write words that are important enough for your daughter's book about what it means to truly live? Words that convey the full depth of the blessing her life has been to you? So, of course, I decided on a movie. They were categorized alphabetically, and I chose one under *A* because I hate it when people take forever to decide what to watch.

The film I clicked on is about a guy who could travel in time. He couldn't go forward; he could only go back, and the choices he made, just like all our choices, always affected his future. That movie turned out to have the same message as this book. Yes, I happened on a film about living life to its fullest. Don't you love it when God answers prayers you didn't even think to ask?

I hope you don't mind this spoiler, but in the end, the main character decides that even though he can go back in time, the best course of action is to simply live each day only once. However, he lives his days differently because of the knowledge he gains. Just before the closing credits, he says, "I've learned the final lesson from my travels in time. . . . I just try to live every day as if I've deliberately come back to this one day, to enjoy it as if it was the full, final day of my extraordinary, ordinary life."[1]

What if you lived each day deliberately, as if it were the full, final day of your extraordinary, ordinary life? What if you lived like this was your only chance at this day? Well, it is. We all know that, of course, but what if you really took hold of the thought that, for better or worse, this is your only chance at this day? How would it change you? Even more than that, what if you saw each of your ordinary days as extraordinary and decided to live each one to its fullest? That's exactly what this book is about.

I don't think there is anyone better suited to write a book about what it means to really live than Sadie. She gives everything she does everything she's got. She laughs a lot and cries when needed; she dances in her bedroom and sings in the shower. She dreams big dreams and actually goes after them. She's not afraid to fail, and when she does, she jumps back up and dusts herself off. She faces her fears and is confident in who God created her to be. She doesn't listen to the haters or let the opinions of others define her. She listens hard to those who love her and is always eager to learn. She seeks the wisdom of those before her and passes on what she has learned to those coming up behind her. She works to make the world a better place and makes sure those around her know without a shadow of a doubt exactly how much she loves them.

I'll never forget her tenth-grade year in high school when she didn't make the cheerleading squad. Sadie has always been super competitive—not the kind of competitive that gets mad when others win but the kind that makes her shoot a hundred free throws every day in the summer to get ready for the next basketball season. The kind of competitive that won't let her quit until she makes all one hundred of them. Honestly, Sadie's hard work usually pays off. This time, though, it didn't. She didn't make the squad. She was sad, and I was sad for her.

A few months later, the cheerleaders were going away to cheer camp. I walked outside to find Sadie recording herself on her phone doing ridiculously funny dances, and I asked her what she was doing. She told me that her friends were nervous about cheer camp because there would be some tough competition. She was making a funny video each day while they were at camp to make them laugh and to encourage them along the way.

Sadie could have been sad, bitter, jealous, or all of the above because her friends were together at cheer camp and she was not. But instead of wallowing in self-pity, she was cheering on the cheerleaders. I loved that moment and will never forget it. She had figured out at a young age what many of us take a lifetime to learn: dwelling on what we didn't get helps no one, and we're happiest when we can celebrate others' successes. (Plus, ridiculous dance moves make everything better!)

The very next year *Dancing with the Stars* asked Sadie to be on the show. She flew out to Hollywood two days later, and within two weeks she was on the dance floor competing for a mirror ball trophy. Life is weird like that. You may think you need something to make your life complete, but God says, "Just wait on Me. I have something better planned for you." It won't always come quickly, but God promises to show up if you will trust in Him. He's done it in my life and in the lives of my friends and family members, and He will do it in yours.

> We're happiest when we can celebrate others' successes.

The guy in the movie learned that going back in time wasn't the answer. The answer lies in living today like you mean it—with gratitude and intention. These lines concluded the movie: "We're all traveling through time together every day of our lives. All we can do is do our best to relish this remarkable ride."[2]

We're all in this together, people. Every one of us is created in the image of God, marked with a purpose, designed with a plan, with gifts and talents that no one else has. We are each known intimately and loved immeasurably by the Creator of the universe. If you don't think your life is remarkable, I pray that, as you read this book, you will think again.

> We're all in this together.

Introduction

LIVE /LIV/*verb*

1. Remain alive.

- Be alive at a specified time.
- To make one's home in a particular place with a particular person.
- Have an exciting or fulfilling life.[3]

F YOU'VE PICKED UP THIS BOOK, IT'S SAFE TO SAY THAT YOU
are alive. You've got a heartbeat and are breathing, but if you're like most of us, maybe you've felt at some point like you weren't really living. Or maybe it goes even deeper than that; maybe you've had times when you didn't even care to live, when simply breathing felt difficult.

When I was younger, I used to carry an inhaler for my brother who had asthma. I never had asthma or trouble with breathing, but he did, and if his lungs ever gave him trouble, I wanted to know I could help. This book is like an inhaler I want to give you. I hope it is a breath of life. For some of you, it will be an exhilarating breath—one of confidence and celebration. For others, I pray it will be the rescue inhaler or the ole breathe-in-and-breathe-out guidance that keeps you going so you can get to that confidence and celebration.

But no matter who you are, if you are alive, this book is for you. This is my third book with the word *live* in the title. The first was *Live Original*; the second was *Live Fearless*. I wanted to call this one simply *Live*. If you were going to read all three of my books, this might just be the one I would tell you to start with. How are we even going to get to the message of living originally or fearlessly if we do not truly know our life is valuable enough to live?

To be vulnerable with you all, I need to share the serious backstory of this book. During the writing process I went on a trip to Oklahoma to speak at one of my favorite churches. I had been excited about it for months. Right before the event I got news that my friend had committed suicide.

I was drying my hair when I received the text, and I dropped my hair dryer in shock and began to weep. I wept for his wife, for his kid, for his friends, and for him. How could this happen? Why did this happen?

The reality is that suicide is the second leading cause of death for people aged fifteen to twenty-four. Nearly eight hundred thousand people a year will make the same devastating choice my friend made. This happens about every forty seconds.[4] I know this book will land in the hands of many people who have had plans, who have written letters, and who are struggling through depression, and because of the anxiety and loneliness, have not talked to anyone about this. Please don't wait until it's too late. Go talk to someone right now: a friend, a counselor, a minister at church. Or call the National Suicide Prevention Lifeline at 1-800-273-8255. I want to give you this book, this breath of life. I am no expert, but I am a good friend, and maybe that is what some of you need right now. You are not alone.

I want to talk about life and death in this book, which I know is an intimidating topic. Life is hard at times, so it is hard to talk about. And death makes us feel sad or afraid, so we don't bring it up. So let's just start with the simplest definition of the verb *live*. As you can see on page xi, the first definition is to "remain alive." Let me ask you: Have you ever thought about how miraculous it is that you are here on earth,

> You are
> not alone.

that you are you? Think of the millions of things that had to happen exactly the way they happened for you to be alive—not to mention for you to be reading this right now. The odds are astounding. A scientist named Dr. Ali Binazir has studied this, and he concluded that the odds of you existing at all are 1 in $10^{2,685,000}$. That number is so unlikely that Dr. Binazir concluded that the chances of being alive are basically *zero*.[5]

I dare say that if you are reading this, you made it past those terrible odds and are indeed remaining alive. The first definition of *live* is nothing to take for granted, but there is so much more. I would love to see us go beyond just the idea of remaining alive to choosing to *live*.

I want you to realize that your being alive is significant and that there is a reason you are here. Even if you feel lifeless, worthless, or empty right now, God has put life in you because there is something in you that this world is craving. You bring something to the table of life that nobody else brings. You are valuable and loved. And I believe, contrary to how you may feel right now, that the life God has for you is exciting and meant to be lived to its fullest. If you're not really feeling it yet, don't worry—we'll get there.

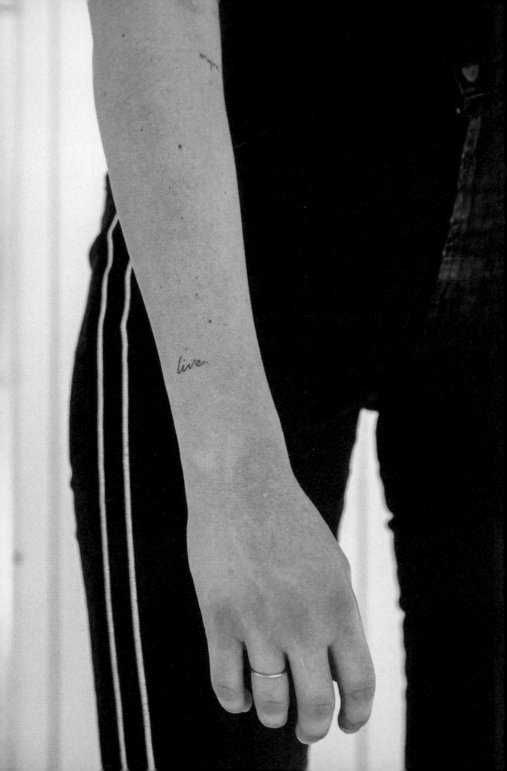

Words

I LOVE WORDS, AND I LIKE TO UNDERSTAND THEM BETTER through their definitions. The ability to use words is something that makes us humans different from any other part of God's creation. In John, Jesus is referred to as "the Word." John 1:1–5 says this:

> In the beginning was the Word, and the Word was with God, and the Word was God. . . . Through him all things were made; without him nothing was made that has been made. In him was life, and that life was the light of all mankind. The light shines in the darkness, and the darkness has not overcome it.

Even if your world feels dark right now, the darkness has not and *never will* overcome the light! Words—the ones we speak over ourselves and over others—are powerful. In this book I want to equip you with some of those words of life.

Let's take a minute and talk about the word *live* and some more definitions of this powerful verb. In addition to "remaining alive," another definition is to "make one's home in a particular place or with a particular person." A synonym for this is *reside*. For our purposes, let's keep it simple by combining those two and saying that to *live* is "to remain and to reside." What does that look like, remaining and residing?

To remain means to "continue to exist, especially after other similar or related people or things have ceased to exist." Maybe you have been trying to remain in things that will not last instead of things that are eternal. Maybe the job you thought would last forever let you go, you had to move, your parents got divorced, your friends left, you broke up, the season changed. The thing you put your security in has crumbled, and now you do not know what your life is. It can be tough to remain when it seems like everything else is falling apart around you. So we need to look at what we are remaining and residing in.

There's an "even when" quality to both definitions, right? To remain alive, we have to continue *even when* things change and circumstances fall apart. Now isn't that something? How do we do that? By remaining in the One who never changes. James 1:17 tells us, "Every good and perfect gift is from above, coming down from the Father of the heavenly lights, who does not change like shifting shadows." Does it feel like the circumstances of your life are constantly changing? Of course it does, because we live in a world of seasons! The things of this life change, so I want to remind you or lead you to remain in God—He is the same yesterday, today, and tomorrow. This is what I have found to be the path of life.

> God is the same yesterday, today, and tomorrow.

The other part of our definition of *live* is "to reside." Because of Jesus, you have a place where you belong. You get to reside in

SAY YES TO LIFE.

God's house forever. Ephesians 2:19–22 (MSG) paints a powerful picture of this:

> You're no longer wandering exiles. This kingdom of faith is now your home country. You're no longer strangers or outsiders. You *belong* here, with as much right to the name Christian as anyone. God is building a home. He's using us all—irrespective of how we got here—in what he is building. He used the apostles and prophets for the foundation. Now he's using you, fitting

you in brick by brick, stone by stone, with Christ Jesus as the cornerstone that holds all the parts together.

Jesus paid it all; He invites you into His Father's house, a safe place to reside.

Maybe you are thinking, *Okay, I got it. I need to remain in God and reside in His house, but how do I really live?*

Because life just happened *for* us and death will happen *to* us, we sometimes forget that we have a part to play in the act of living. There's this whole spiritual realm happening, but how do we live right here, right now, with all the problems of today?

> How do we live right here, right now, with all the problems of today?

It's hard to understand when our hearts are weighed down with the things that drain life away. The world tells us we'll find life in other people's approval, in achievement, in exercising more or eating better, or by changing our makeup or hairstyle. It says we'll find life in all sorts of things that don't last or have any eternal value. It's understandable that when people base their lives on these things, which aren't God Himself, they feel like death is breathing in their faces. I know the feeling. It's something that happens to all of us, no matter who you are, how old you are, or where you are in faith or life.

I will encourage you throughout this book to live in your solid identity in Jesus and to say no to lies that your identity is in anything less. Live with purposeful direction and say no to cheap copies or temporary fixes. Live in the community of people around you and find a way to live fully and joyfully with them and in your God-given place among them. Say yes to life and find out how it can be so much more than remaining alive. Keep reading—because it's time for you to truly *live*.

Where Life Is Found

WHEN I STARTED WRITING THIS BOOK, I KNEW THERE WAS one Bible story I wanted to begin with. Before I jump into it, let me tell you a story about the story.

I told it to a group of women in prison. Most of them had never heard it before. The room was silent as I shared, and the women were captivated by the truth they were hearing. As I spoke, they began to weep. They were so deeply touched by the message of this story, and it gave them so much hope that, after I left the prison that day, I knew I had to go back to it personally, seeking to understand why it had such an impact on those women.

Now I'd like to reimagine this Bible story with you (and I've taken a lot of creative liberties!).

There was a father with two daughters. The girls were at that teenager stage, right before becoming young adults—about the time to prepare for where they would go after school. The funny thing about these two girls was that they were as different as they could possibly be—so different that people wondered if they were actually related. Sometimes people in families are like that. Can I get an amen?

When the sisters were young, the father told them that he would invest in their lives when they became adults by giving each of them a share of his wealth. The oldest sister thought her father's offer was extremely kind and appreciated the financial provision he made for her. She always had a mature way of preparing for her future. She was definitely the saver in the family. She was content with her life as it was, so she saved her money, stayed close to her family, and planned to work in the family business.

The younger sister did not have the same reaction to her father's generous offer. She had always been the spender in the family—always wanting the next best thing. She saw it as her "ticket to Hollywood," so to speak. The day she turned eighteen, she set out to live the life she had craved for years. She was living large and wild as she blew her father's money left and right. Every morning she woke up blasting hype music, thinking, *I'm young and rich. These are the best years of my life. I can—and should—do anything and everything I want to do.* With that mind-set guiding her, as you can imagine, she recklessly wasted money on the next best trend to stay relevant. Her life was filled with alcohol, drugs, and partying all night until the sun came up the next morning—just to make sure she didn't miss out on anything and no one forgot about her.

After some time of this unsustainable lifestyle, she eventually ran out of money and did not have any sort of education or career path to fall back on. She quickly realized that her so-called friends liked her only because she bought their meals, planned fun trips, and gave them expensive gifts. She found herself alone. When she ran out of money for even the basics like food and rent, she was

faced with the reality that if she did not go home, she didn't know how she would survive. She had no one to call and nowhere to go.

Her shame could not let her linger on the thought of home for long, so she searched for a job anywhere she could find one. She was so desperate, she found herself in situations that just a year earlier she would have said she would rather die than live through. She was doing things she never thought she would do for money, but she felt she had no other choice. She lost her identity and her home.

She had lost everything but her very breath. She even contemplated suicide because she was so exhausted, lonely, and filled with shame over wasting everything her father had given her. She did not want to continue down the road she was on, but she couldn't see a way out.

The weaker and more tired she became, the more she began to think about her family. She thought about the heartbreak she must have caused her father and mother. She wondered what her sister must have thought of her. She began having bitter thoughts, comparing herself to her sister, thinking, *Why could I not have been more like her?* She knew she had broken her mom's heart.

She got lost in painful thoughts of her family sitting comfortably at home, criticizing her for the way she had chosen to live. *Do they even think of me at all?* she pondered. She thought about all the people who worked for her father as she was growing up. They were a wealthy family, so they had people who cooked for them and cleaned for them. She thought about her dad's assistant, who would answer his calls, drive her and her sister to school, and run to the store for him when he needed. "Even they were better off!" she cried as her thoughts became so loud that these words burst out of her mouth. The back-and-forth in her mind was growing intense.

As she reminded herself of her stupidity and stubbornness, she began to weep. *Look at me*, she thought to herself. *I am no longer worthy to be my father's daughter. I am not even fit to be a member of my family, because of all the bad choices I have made. But I have to go home, or I am not going to live. I will go back and ask Dad if I can work for him. At this point, I would be glad just to scrub the floor of what used to be my home.*

As she made her way back home on foot, like the people she used to pass in her nice car, she rehearsed what she would say when she saw her family—and wondered what they would think of her when they saw her. She grew more and more anxious. Her heart was pounding. She even considered heading back to her terrible job to take another night shift, but the thought of residing in that old place one more night kept her going.

When she got back to her hometown, before going to her family's neighborhood, she decided to sit at the coffee shop where she would often go when she felt lost on what she used to consider a hard day. She felt she needed a little more time to muster up the courage to press past the weight of her guilt.

She was almost to her regular spot when she looked up and, to her absolute shock, saw her dad. Her heart felt as though it had dropped to her gut. She knew she was too close to turn around. Her dad saw her, and in the most beautiful, heartwarming tone and with tear-filled eyes, he simply said, "My daughter, you came back home!"

> You were dead, but now you are alive. You were lost, but now you are found.

Before she knew it, she was wrapped in her dad's arms with his tears falling on her. She asked with a shaky, anxious voice, "Why are you here?" He replied, "Do you remember when you were young and I told you girls that if you ever got lost, you should stay right where I saw you last, and I would come back and find you? Whenever I would see you here, I would pray that you would know you are not alone in whatever heartache you were feeling. I've come here every day since you've left. I've been waiting here for you to come back to where I saw you last. Now you are here. Let's go home."

As overwhelmed as she was by this, she said, "No, Dad. Stop. You don't know what I have done. I've messed up. I have sinned against you, and I've sinned against God. I am not pure. I am not clean. I am not even sure who I am anymore. I have no place here. I don't deserve to be your daughter or to be in this perfect family or belong to this home. I came back to work. I am no longer worthy of this kind of love."

The father stopped for a moment and pulled out his phone. He called his wife and excitedly told her their daughter was found. She was surprised to hear him tell her mom to cook her favorite meal—chicken quesadillas with chips and guacamole. He called his assistant to get some new clothes for his girl and have them laid out on the bed, ready for her when they arrived. He sent a text out to the family to come over quickly. He was throwing a party to celebrate—his daughter was home!

She stood there in shock at his response despite all she had told him. She stopped him and said,

> You are forgiven, and you are altogether beautiful.

"But you're not mad?" He then looked at his daughter and said, "Daughter, you were dead, but now you are alive. You were lost, but now you are found. You are my daughter. Nothing you could ever do can change that. I am so sorry for all that has happened to you and all that has been done to you. You are safe now. You are forgiven, and you are altogether beautiful. This has always been your home, to remain and reside in forever."

HOME

Here are lyrics to a song I wrote one day when I was finding my way back home.

Every promise that You made
Is still the same for me today
I don't have to hold on to fear
I know I can trust what I hear

When You say *family* and *forever*
You mean every word You say
I know You won't change the locks on me
I can trust Your loyalty

In Your open house
There's not a sense to strive for love
I can rest and know
That every single word is true
In Your open house
Everything I lost was found
I can call this home
It's so free to know I'm known

You saw every little thing
And still came running after me
I didn't have to do a thing
You always wanted me for me

Then You spoke over me
The life for me that I could not see
You gave me love I can't deny
I never have to run and hide
You are everything
You are everything
You are everything that I need
You are everything that I need
And I am sorry for anything in between
You're everything I need
I can call this home
I feel so free to know I'm known

From *Know* to *Realize*

I THINK THAT BECAUSE WE KNOW CERTAIN BIBLE STORIES SO well, we sometimes do not realize how life changing they are. When we realize that they are not only stories but pictures of what can be real for us, it will change the way we see our lives.

That's why I started this book with a retelling of Jesus' story of the prodigal son from the gospel of Luke. So many of us know this story, but we may fail to realize the power in it.

To *know* something means "to have information in your mind,"[6] while to *realize* something means "to understand a situation, sometimes suddenly" or "to achieve something you were hoping for."[7] Knowing something is quite different from realizing it. When I shared the story of the prodigal son in the women's prison, I watched them realize that there is something for them to fulfill in life. I saw it reshape their perspective of who God is as a loving Father and saw hope begin to rise in that room of women living behind bars.

I personalized this story in the last chapter, but it's important to see it as the Bible portrays it, so let's look at that now.

You may have picked up this book having known your whole life that there is a God and that He is your Father, yet you have lived with the mentality that you are alone, afraid, and missing true value and quality in your life. Maybe you have not realized all that this story offers you and that your reason to keep living is that you have a purpose to fulfill. Or maybe you have never believed in God and have never read Scripture before. Maybe you have never thought much about life at all. But as your eyes wander across these words of life, you are embarking on an exciting journey of getting to know something and then having the full realization of how incredible it is. These are the words Jesus spoke:

> There was a man who had two sons. The younger one said to his father, "Father, give me my share of the estate." So he divided his property between them.
>
> Not long after that, the younger son got together all he had, set off for a distant country and there squandered his wealth in wild living. After he had spent everything, there was a severe famine in that whole country, and he began to be in need. So he went and hired himself out to a citizen of that country, who sent him to his fields to feed pigs. He longed to fill his stomach with the pods that the pigs were eating, but no one gave him anything.
>
> When he came to his senses, he said, "How many of my father's hired servants have food to spare, and here I am starving to death! I will set out and go back

IF YOU'VE GIVEN
YOUR LIFE TO GOD,
YOU ALREADY
HAVE ALL YOU
NEED TO FILL
YOUR HEART
AND SOUL.

to my father and say to him: Father, I have sinned against heaven and against you. I am no longer worthy to be called your son; make me like one of your hired servants." So he got up and went to his father.

But while he was still a long way off, his father saw him and was filled with compassion for him; he ran to his son, threw his arms around him and kissed him.

The son said to him, "Father, I have sinned against heaven and against you. I am no longer worthy to be called your son."

But the father said to his servants, "Quick! Bring the best robe and put it on him. Put a ring on his finger and sandals on his feet. Bring the fattened calf and kill it. Let's have a feast and celebrate. For this son of mine was dead and is alive again; he was lost and is found." So they began to celebrate. (Luke 15:11–24)

In this story we see the prodigal son move from knowing to realizing. Actually, he realized something he already knew: his father had a house and servants who had food to spare when he was on the verge of losing his life (Luke 15:17).

Remember, to live is to *remain* and to *reside*. When we try to remain and reside in things that fade away, we are contradicting the action of living.

Sometimes when we're trying to live our lives fully, we go wrong by turning to quick, temporary highs. We try to satisfy ourselves through things that will leave us high and dry instead of simply filling our lives with the promises of God, which are guaranteed. We try to fill the empty spaces in our hearts, the gaps in our lives. The expression "fill the gaps" means "to add to what is needed to something to make it complete"[8] or "to serve temporarily."[9] To say that a gap needs filling is to say that from the beginning something is missing, but I'm telling you, if you've given your life to God, you already have all you need to fill your heart and soul; you just have to realize it. To fill a gap, you have to add something to it so that there is enough, but to fulfill something, you simply need to step into its reality.

> If you've given your life to God, you have all you need.

To the prodigal son, filling the gap meant prostitutes and partying. What has filling the gaps meant for you? Has it looked like these:

- Diet pills to make you feel beautiful?
- Sleeping around to make you feel loved?
- Editing your pictures or sending inappropriate photos to make your body look good enough to be seen or liked?
- Pornography to make you feel satisfied?
- Addiction to make you feel numb?

If you are involved in these activities, have you found that you cannot stop because the rush is the only thing that keeps you going? Have you discovered that they always end in pain, fear, emptiness, and feelings of worthlessness? If I'm describing you, I want to tell you this: you are not worthless, but those things are *worth* so much *less* than who you are.

- You are already loved just as you are.
- You are already enough just as you are.
- You are already seen just as you are.
- You are already known just as you are.

Because:

- God is love.

- God is enough.
- God created you, formed you, and is with you for His satisfaction just because you are His.

This is your reality—not because of what you have done or what you will do but simply because of who you are and where you belong. It's time to get back the fullness of your life.

The minute the prodigal son stepped into reality is the moment he was met with the most overwhelming realization of his life's worth. Though we will never have a full perspective of what God will do with our lives on this side of heaven, we get glimpses of His immense love for us in hearing Jesus tell this story of the prodigal son and fully grasping the love of the Father. First Corinthians 2:9 tells us, "No eye has seen, no ear has heard, and no mind has imagined what God has prepared for those who love him" (NLT).

> It's time to get back the fullness of your life.

It's time to realize who your Father is. You might be thinking, though, *Sadie, I feel like I am eating with the pigs. I'm the girl throwing my life away. How do I get back home from here?* I'll offer you one tidbit of advice that will carry you through this book and through life. It's only four words, so don't miss it:

Turn in His direction.

The turning point is where everything changes. There is a path of death and a path of life. So turn in His direction, toward life.

From *About*
to *For*

ONCE LED A SEVEN-WEEK BIBLE STUDY FOR GIRLS IN A juvenile detention center—"juvie" for short. During the fifth week, I asked them, "What changes do you hope to see in yourself when we finish our study?"

The first girl said, "I don't want to be so mean anymore." When she said that, everyone started laughing because she was so mean to all of them all the time. They began joking with her, making comments such as, "Yeah, right. Who are you if you aren't mean?"

I finally intervened, saying, "Whoa. Whoa. Everyone chill. All of you, tell her you believe it will happen for her." Still laughing, and not really believing it, they said to her, "I believe that for you."

The next girl took the challenge more seriously than I expected. She said, "When I am done with this, I do not want to go back to drugs." The other girls knew exactly how to respond. All the voices in the room were clear as they said somberly, "I believe that for you."

I BELIEVE THAT

FOR YOU.

One girl after another shared how she wanted to change, mentioning what she wanted to turn away from and what she wanted to turn toward. They each allowed themselves the opportunity to get past what they believed *about* themselves and *about* each other so they could believe *for* themselves and *for* each other.

Sometimes what stops us from journeying back home on the path of life is what we believe about ourselves, especially when our mistakes have led us into places we never thought we'd be, and shame makes it hard for us to believe good things are in store for our future.

What do you think the prodigal son thought about himself when he was eating the pigs' food? I'm not sure, but it probably wasn't good. I believe the reason it was so hard for him to imagine his dad welcoming him back home was that he struggled to get past what he believed *about* himself and couldn't even begin to believe something *for* himself.

The same thing happens to people all the time, maybe even you. It's happened to me before. If you let what you believe about yourself—and what other people believe about you—define your life, that would be a tragedy. You'll never find out what you're capable of. But your life can change the world when you start believing good things for yourself.

What God believes *for* you is probably different than what you believe for yourself. Are you ready to move *for*ward? The story of the prodigal son shows us how God loves

> If you let what you believe about yourself—and what other people believe about you—define your life, you'll never find out what you're capable of.

us before we even make our way back to Him. He is ready to help us turn in His direction. With that in mind, read this verse again: "So he got up and went to his father. But

Turn your heart toward Him and step onto the path of life.

while he was still a long way off, his father saw him and was filled with compassion for him; he ran to his son, threw his arms around him and kissed him" (Luke 15:20).

Before the son ever said a word, explained himself, or began to apologize, his father made sure he knew he was loved and welcome at home.

The father in the story moves forward quickly. He does not waste a moment starting the celebration. The son did not have to strive for it or work for it. All it took for him was to go back home. I assure you that God the Father moves forward quickly too. When He sees that you want to come home to Him, He will get the party started. All it takes is for you to turn your heart toward Him and step onto the path of life.

This depiction of God may be contrary to your idea of who He is. Maybe your religious experience has told you that once you mess up, you can't turn back to Him. Maybe your friends gave you that impression, or maybe you came to believe it some other way. The truth is that when God sees you turning toward Him, making your way back home, before you even say a word, He will say, "Welcome home, child."

Knowing your identity as a child of a good Father, what have you been believing *about* yourself that you want to let go of? What do you want to believe *for* yourself?

There was a time in my life when I felt lost and far away from home (not my physical home, but spiritually speaking). The things I believed about myself were keeping me from where I am now. I believed that, because of some insecurities, mistakes, and bad judgments, I was disqualified from doing the things I had once felt called to do for God—to write, speak, and preach His Word. I could not imagine that He would welcome me back to His house and clothe me in His best. Now I'm writing my third book, so I was able to move past that old belief and go forward with God.

> What do you
> want to believe
> *for* yourself?

These are the truths I had to start believing, and you can believe them too.

1. I am forgiven (Colossians 3:13).
2. I am redeemed (Romans 3:23–25).
3. I am loved (John 3:16).
4. I am lovely (Song of Songs 4:7).
5. I am pure (Psalm 51:10; Isaiah 1:18).
6. I am welcome in God's house (John 14:2).

You've Got Options

ADMIT IT. I LOVE TO KNOW ALL MY OPTIONS. EVEN WITH something as simple as a meal, I want to know what my choices are. I *will* eat. I just want to think through all the restaurants that are available. When I get there, I even ask the waiter what he or she thinks the best option is for my meal. I'm the same way about life. I think the best kind of life is one that is open to all possibilities. Let me encourage you: Keep your mind open. Keep your heart open. Don't ever shut down an idea or an option too soon. For example, I have a friend who often says no to opportunities or invitations because it would require her to make more effort than she often wants to make. That girl can say no to a great idea faster than anybody. But if I ask her to think about it and to consider how much she might enjoy it, she almost always changes her mind and says yes. And then, of course, she's glad she did it.

The power to make choices is a gift from God. You never know where something can take you. A willingness to think about and then act on something you haven't thought of before can take your life to a whole new level.

There's one decision I've already made, though, and I don't need to think about it anymore. I know the options, and I've landed. You see, there's only one basic choice people need to make, and that's the choice between life and death. Those are our two bottom-line options, and what we decide determines everything about how to live.

Most of the time, when people talk about life and death, they're speaking in physical terms. They're talking about whether people have a heartbeat, whether their brains are working, and whether they can breathe on their own. If all these organs are functioning, they say a person is alive. When the heart, brain, lungs, kidneys, and other organs fail, a person is dead—technically.

But when I use the words *life* and *death* in this book, I'm talking about something different and beyond the physical realm. I'm talking about the quality of the spiritual, emotional, relational force inside you and whether that leads to happiness, hope, light, strength, confidence, purpose, passion, success, peace, and fulfillment (life) or whether it leads to misery, despair, darkness, weakness, insecurity, worthlessness, apathy, failure, and feeling restless and unfulfilled (death).

I'm a girl who likes options, and I've found the only one that leads to life. Jesus talks about it in the Sermon on the Mount: "Enter through the narrow gate. For wide is the gate and broad is the road that leads to destruction, and many enter through it. But small is the gate and narrow the road that leads to life, and only a few find it" (Matthew 7:13–14).

Later, at the end of His life, Jesus told His disciples He wouldn't be with them much longer. He said, "My Father's house has many rooms; if that were not so, would I have told you that I am going there to prepare a place for you? And if I go and prepare a place for you, I will come back and take you to be with me that you also may be where I am" (John 14:2–3). Thomas wasn't sure about that (they don't call him "Doubting Thomas" for nothing) and said, "Lord, we don't know where you are going, so how can we know the way?" (v. 5). Then Jesus answered, "I am the way and the truth and the life" (v. 6). Jesus is always an option! You can choose life through Him.

Everyone has to make the same choice for life, whether they know it or not. One of the saddest things I encounter is when I hear about people who have made bad choices and ended up in a terrible situation simply because they didn't know they had another option. They put themselves on a path of pain, difficulty, and destruction because they didn't know they could choose freedom, happiness, destiny, purpose, fulfillment, and peace. One reason I wrote this book is so that doesn't happen to you and so you can tell others it doesn't have to happen to them.

I want you to know that you have a choice! You can decide whether to pursue life or death. Look at what God says about it: "Today I have given you the choice between life and death, between blessings and curses. Now I call on heaven and earth to witness the choice you make. Oh, that you would *choose life*, so that you and your descendants might *live*!" (Deuteronomy 30:19 NLT). Part of what I like about this verse is that God is saying, "These are your options—life or death, blessings or curses." Then He tells us exactly what He wants us to do. It's almost like He is begging us to make the right decision when He says, "Oh, that you would choose life!"

You know that feeling you have when you go to take a test and you study hard ahead of time so you will know the answers? Then when you see the questions and know the answers, you're thinking, *I'm crushing this*. This whole thing about life and death is similar. God has given you the answer. He's already said, "Choose life"!

Life *is* an option. Change *is* possible.

Like a good preacher would say, "Read it again!"

Life *is* an option. Change *is* possible.

Turn Up the Contrast

ONE NIGHT I WAS AT A CONFERENCE, AND THE SPEAKER SAID something that really hit my core. She said that as believers, we are called to be people of contrast. I have thought about this a lot, and I think she meant that when we are living as people of the light, our lives will look different than the lives of people who live according to the world's values.

When I think of contrast, I think of the edit function in the Instagram toolbox. We spend a lot of time editing photos to get the contrast to the right percentage even though no one would ever notice the difference in our pictures unless we turned the contrast all the way up. No one would do that, of course, because it would be way too noticeable. This made me think about how I spent so much time on many things that don't really make a difference or create change—time I spent worrying about things I couldn't change, filling my mind with things that aren't positive, watching shows that aren't beneficial to me, and listening to music that didn't leave me inspired.

The next day, I started weeding that time out of my life. Instead, I spent more time investing in the ones who made me grow, learning from ones who are way ahead of me on life's journey, listening to things that inspire me, and reading things that change my perspective in a positive way.

Choosing to spend my time differently freed my mind from thinking of the things I used to worry about. I started seeing a difference and being a cultivator of change. I could no longer justify spending so much time on things that only made me blend into a sea of twenty-first-century people who all have the same thought: there *has* to be something more.

People are afraid of being different and standing for what they believe. Many are scared to be seen claiming Christianity. If that's you, I would encourage you by saying that, in Christianity, the focus isn't on you. It's about who God is in you. It's not about you being seen but about people being able to notice the difference that happens within you. Let me assure you that who you are in the name of Jesus and who you will become when you step out of the limitations the world has put on you and into a kingdom mind-set is *nothing* to be ashamed of! When people see you, they will see freedom, peace, joy, love, grace, beauty, and the kindness the world is longing for. What your life displays will shine in contrast to what the world is used to seeing.

> There *has* to be something more.

Let me encourage you today to be bold enough to turn up the contrast. The results aren't up to you; they're up to God. And the world may be hungrier to see the contrast than you think, because Romans 8:19 says, "For the creation waits in eager expectation for

HOW ARE YOU

SPENDING YOUR

TIME?

the children of God to be revealed." I'm determined to live as a person of contrast. Want to join me?

Keep a log of the ways you spend your time this week, and ask yourself for each item, *Is this helping me live the life I want to live? Is this helping me grow?* Then think of the ways you want to grow—the direction you want to go. What good contrast do you want to make in the world? Do you want to be generous in a world that withholds? Kind in a world that makes fun? Deep in a world that's shallow? All about relationships in a world that's all about advancement? Start looking for ways to spend your precious time on activities that educate, expand, and encourage you—things that give you *life* instead of death. Make little choices today to turn up the contrast.

> Be bold enough to turn up the contrast.

What's That You Say?

ONE TIME WHEN CHRISTIAN AND I WERE DATING, WE WENT out for a walk, which we love to do, but we found ourselves in an argument. I was telling him something I wished that he would have remembered to do, and his response was, "I suck." When those words came out of his mouth, I got so upset. I had shared with him before that it really makes me sad when he speaks negative things over himself. Well, this conversation just kept going downhill and ended with me saying, "That is it. You walk that way. I'm walking this way." As I turned to walk away, Christian said, "You said you would never walk away." As I type this, I see how dramatic we were both being, but thinking back on this story, I cannot help but question why Christian and I both said and did things that neither of us truly meant or believed.

I remember hearing a cheer at a football game that

> Do your words bring life or death?

started with a group of people yelling something for another group to act out; the other group yelled in response, "What's that you say?" and then the first group repeated what they said and proceeded to do that action.

"What's that you say?" is a *great* question. Being challenged about what we say is helpful because it makes us think about whether we are confident in the words we speak. Sometimes we say things we don't really mean. Stopping to think about whether we would repeat them can cause us to examine what's in our hearts and make sure our words align with it, and then make sure our words and our heart align with our actions.

So I want to ask you today, "What's that you say?" I mean, what are you talking about—to yourself and to others? What kinds of actions are your words sparking? Are they bringing life or death? Are you even confident in what you are saying?

Now I want to offer you a visual, so to speak, of what the words of life and the words of death look like:

The words of life **empower**. The words of death destroy.

The words of life **encourage**. The words of death cause people to lose heart.

The words of life **affirm**. The words of death tear down.

The words of life give **hope**. The words of death cause despair.

The words of life are **confident**. The words of death are powerless.

The words of life are **full of hope** for the future. The words of death replay the pain of the past.

But wait. There's more. Let's go a little deeper. Just as a tree has roots that run deep underground, the words you speak have a root

EXAMINE WHAT'S IN YOUR HEART AND MAKE SURE YOUR WORDS ALIGN WITH IT.

system too. You can look at a tree and see if it's healthy or not by looking at what it produces. If it's leafy and green and full of good fruit, you can bet it has a strong root system. If it's dry and brown, its roots aren't nourishing it as they should. Likewise, you can figure out what your root system is by the fruit of your lips—the words you say (Hebrews 13:15). Let's look at some common roots of life and death.

The words of life are rooted in a place of **security**. The words of death are rooted in a place of jealousy.

The words of life are rooted in knowing you're **loved**. The words of death come from feeling unwanted.

The words of life are rooted in feeling **content**. The words of death come from never being satisfied.

The words of life are rooted in being **confident** in who God made you to be. The words of death come from striving to do more to find your worth.

The words of life are rooted in **knowing** you are accepted just the way you are. The words of death come from feeling rejection.

The words of life are rooted in **peace**. The words of death come from fear and anxiety.

The words of life are rooted in a **positive attitude**. The words of death come from a negative outlook.

The words of life are rooted in **caring** about others. The words of death come from focusing on yourself.

It's important to look at what your words are rooted in so you can be confident in knowing how they impact you and how they affect others.

What's the Tea?

THE CONSTITUTION OF THE UNITED STATES OF AMERICA GIVES citizens the right to freedom of speech and protects it in the First Amendment. So we're clear, here's what it says in fancy Constitution language:

> Congress shall make no law respecting an establishment of religion, or prohibiting the free exercise thereof; or abridging the freedom of speech, or of the press; or the right of the people peaceably to assemble, and to petition the Government for a redress of grievances.[10]

It's clear, all right. In America, people are free to speak their minds. I'm thankful for that and the other protections our Constitution gives us. I'm all for the *freedom* to speak, but I'm also in favor of using *wisdom* when we say things.

Believe it or not, this debate about what people should or shouldn't say has been going on for centuries. Even the apostle Paul commented on it: "'I have the right to do anything,' you say—but not everything is beneficial. 'I have the right to do anything'—but not everything is constructive" (1 Corinthians 10:23).

Everyone in my generation needs to hear this: *not everything we want to say is beneficial.*

Maybe you know about modern-day tea parties. These aren't the kind of tea parties our grandmothers went to—where ladies dressed up and drank hot tea and ate sandwiches with no crusts and talked about polite things. No, we have lost the class in our "tea parties." We've given them a bad name. They happen when some-one says, "Let's have a tea party, and I'll spill the tea."

"Spilling the tea" is code for sharing a juicy piece of information, telling people everything that has been going on with you, or pro-viding the background story on something happening with others. It can be tempting to be the one to spill the tea, especially if we are feeling insecure and want to put the negative attention on another. For some reason we think it will make us feel better about ourselves to talk badly about someone else. What I'm talking about here is gossip, and there is no life there.

People like to be "in the know," and they like to be the first to tell others something considered really good information. The problem is that "really good information" isn't always really good for everyone to know, especially if it's a rumor. If it's not true, it could really hurt someone. It could ruin a person's reputation. It could cause pain in a relationship. It could do all kinds of damage you never intended or even thought about when you were just passing along a tidbit. Even if it is true, it may not be something other people need to know.

The wise and mature thing to do when you hear something and think you just can't wait to share it is to ask yourself, *If this situation were happening in my life, would I want the whole world to know about it?* If you wouldn't, then sharing it with others would not be beneficial. If you have some tea, resist the urge to spill it. Knowing how you feel, what you think, or what you heard will not always be helpful to other people. If you have to do something with the tea, just sip on it quietly. That may not sound like a lot of fun, but it would be wise, and wisdom leads to life.

I think we should bring some class back to our tea parties. Choose your words carefully because they have the power of life and death. If we really believe that, it will change the way we speak to other people. God's Word is pretty clear about the power of our words and what we are to do with our speech:

> Don't use foul or abusive language. Let everything you say be good and helpful, so that your words will be an encouragement to those who hear them. (Ephesians 4:29 NLT)

> The tongue can bring death or life; those who love to talk will reap the consequences. (Proverbs 18:21 NLT)

> If you want to enjoy life and see many happy days, keep your tongue from speaking evil and your lips from telling lies. (1 Peter 3:10 NLT)

> The soothing tongue is a tree of life, but a perverse tongue crushes the spirit. (Proverbs 15:4)

> Without wood a fire goes out; without a gossip a quarrel dies down. (Proverbs 26:20)

Negative self-talk or "spilling the tea" is so easy to do, and the Enemy tries to get us to believe that our words have no power, that they don't affect our thoughts and moods and actions. But they do. If we truly believe our words have the power of life and death, we will also be careful about the way we speak not only to others but to ourselves. You know what I'm talking about. Do you ever make a mistake and say to yourself, "I'm so stupid"? Or do you ever look at someone else—someone you think is smarter, more attractive, or more together than you are—and say to yourself, "I'll never have what she has"? This kind of negative self-talk is not innocent. It can be dangerous because words are powerful.

> Our words have the power of life and death.

Let me encourage you to start saying positive things about yourself. Maybe you don't think you're the most beautiful person on earth, but you can look at the mirror and say to yourself, "I really do have a great smile" or "My hair has been looking great!" You can even use Bible verses to talk to yourself. Based on Philippians 4:13 (NKJV), you can say, "I can do all things through Christ who strengthens me." Or you can use Jeremiah 29:11 and say, "Things may be a little tough for me right now, but God knows the plans He has for me, and they are good. He is giving me hope and a future!" You get to decide what you say to yourself. That's part of what it means to have the power of life and death in your tongue.

It's trendy right now to say, "Oooooh, this gives me life!" about something—usually something funny—that gives you a little rush or makes you feel cool. I've said it at times too, but I think it's important to know what actually does give us life. Let's be real: when your life is on the line physically, you are not going to grab an Advil. It may make you feel better, but it's not going to give you life. A little pain relief does not equal real life!

I've experienced this firsthand. I used to try to go out with friends, get a new outfit (or new boyfriend), or change my hair. Unfortunately,

I did some of these things in front of a large, public audience. Thank God, He's a Redeemer! When I tried those things, I was happy for a moment and even had fun. But not until I truly connected with the source of life did I ever really live. When I say "connected with the source of life," I don't mean a scroll on social media. I mean a deep dive in the Word. I went from looking for life in places that could never deliver it in its fullness (because they were not designed to) to a consistent connection to joy.

The thing about a momentary rush is that temporary sources of life always run out. They quickly lose their appeal and aren't life-giving anymore. But there are things that will last for eternity, things we can always count on. These are the things of God, the fruit of who He is: love, joy, peace, patience, kindness, goodness, faithfulness, gentleness, and self-control (Galatians 5:22–23).

PSALM 1:1-6

I love the way Psalm 1 contrasts life and death. It truly teaches us to live. It tells us what to do and what not to do if we want to be firmly rooted in life and flourish—like a healthy, fruit-bearing tree. The key is for us to find our "pleasure and passion" in staying "true to the Word of 'I Am'" (Psalm 1:2 TPT).

Are you living a life that is true to the Word of God? It is a lamp to your feet and a light to your path (Psalm 119:105), which means it will always lead you in the right direction.

Look at Psalm 1:1–6 (TPT) today—soak it in—and let it inspire you.

What delight comes to the one who follows God's ways!
He won't walk in step with the wicked,
nor share the sinner's way,
nor be found sitting in the scorner's seat.

His pleasure and passion is remaining true to the Word
    of "I Am,"
meditating day and night in the true revelation of light.

He will be standing firm like a flourishing tree
planted by God's design,
deeply rooted by the brooks of bliss,
bearing fruit in every season of his life.
He is never dry, never fainting,
ever blessed, ever prosperous.

But how different are the wicked.
All they are is dust in the wind—
driven away to destruction!

The wicked will not endure the day of judgment,
for God will not defend them.
Nothing they do will succeed or endure for long,
for they have no part with those who walk in truth.

But how different it is for the righteous!
The Lord embraces their paths as they move forward
while the way of the wicked leads only to doom.

Lessons from Five and Eighty-Five

ONE OF THE THINGS I LOVE ABOUT MY LIFE IS THAT I HAVE friends and family members of just about every age and stage you can imagine, from very young to—well, I won't say "very old," but I'll say, "people who have lived quite a long time." Every time I interact with them, I see something beautiful and learn something new. If I were to share everything I've learned from my friends and family, it could take up the rest of the book. So I'll just tell you a little about what I've learned from my youngest friends and end with what I've learned from my oldest—my great-grandmother, Mamaw Jo.

It's nice to have five-year-old friends.

They keep it real.

They keep you real.

They keep perspective real.

They keep life real.

They don't even know how not to be real.

I appreciate that. Many of us start doubting what's "real" as we become older—especially in today's time of social media, filters, edits, captions, makeup, and just your old-fashioned two-faced friend. How do you know what is real and what is not? We feel a hunger and craving for authenticity but also a massive fear of being authentic, of showing our true selves.

> Focus on what's real.

I have some five-year-old friends and cousins, and I really enjoy hanging out with them. They have shown me the value of simply being real. They have purified my perspective. And they have taken me back to the simplicity of being a friend.

As I think about my young friends, I realize they have taught me five important life lessons. I hope these take you back to when you were young and ready to conquer the world.

1 Live in the moment.

One day, two five-year-olds—children of some friends of mine—were at my house, and these two cuties asked me to play with them. We started to pretend we were worship leaders. Their parents are all worship leaders, so that's a pretty common game we play. And it is so stinking cute!

Of course, the first thing anyone watching wants to do is take a video. But as soon as someone pulled out a phone, my little buddy said these words, which convicted me: "No, we are not supposed to take pictures. We are just supposed to sing."

We. Are. Just. Supposed. To. Sing.

My young friend knew so much more about life than the adults in the room did that day. There is so much freedom to living in the moment. Why do we have to stop moments to snap a picture? Sometimes by doing that, we actually miss the essence of the moment, and we forget to sing. There are some friends I have more pictures with than memories. These five-year-old children and I have hundreds of memories together and only one picture—which happened to be captured in a single moment when both of them ran into my arms for a big group hug. I love this picture because it wasn't planned, staged, stopped, or filtered and because the moment could not have gotten any better. It was a priceless moment captured in action. These kids don't need a picture to capture the moment. They just live in it.

I love taking pictures, and I come from a family of photographers, so I'm not hating on pictures. This is just a reminder to not let the picture-taking rob you of life's precious moments. Think about whether you're taking a picture for the purpose of showing it off or cherishing a memory. We need to stop thinking so much about the social media value of a photograph and start thinking more about the actual value of the experience. All we're really supposed to do is *just sing*.

> There is so much freedom to living in the moment.

2 Surround yourself with laughter and the people you love, and your day will be a good one.

My five-year-old friends and I all had a sleepover at their grand-parents' house (my friends are cousins), and it was one of the most priceless nights. In the middle of the night, I was awoken by giggles of pure excitement. They couldn't contain their joy.

They dozed off eventually, but two hours later they woke up again and said, "Sadie, why is the night taking so long to be over? I'm ready to play."

I held them off until 3:45 a.m., but their excitement was real. So I woke up long before the sun came up; we watched a movie, and it was one of the best mornings ever—even if it did start at 3:45. The previous day had not been a good one for me. I was pretty upset over some things and had planned to just sleep the day away. Here's the thing: sleeping the day away will not make your bad day good, but waking up, surrounding yourself with good people, expecting a good day, and just simply giggling at the pure joy of being alive may turn your bad day into a good one.

> Surround yourself with good people. Expect a good day. And giggle at the pure joy of being alive.

When was the last time you couldn't wait until morning? Now that's really living.

3 Let people know how happy you are to see them. You may just make their day!

One of my favorite things—one that makes me smile just typing this—is when my little cousin Judson or my little friend Cruce (who are also five but not the same five-year-olds I've already mentioned) sees me and screams, "Sadieeeee!" then runs, arms wide open, to give me the biggest hug. These five-year-olds appreciate the moments in life we sometimes forget to appreciate as we grow older. The little moments are meant to be enjoyed, but sometimes we are too stressed trying to get to the big moments in life that we let things slip by—like seeing someone you love, who you haven't seen in a while, and letting it pass right on by without much fanfare.

Five-year-olds bring joy into the moments of life simply through their little positive spirits, big smiles, and random giggles. They give big hugs just because big hugs are fun and make you feel good. Maybe it's time we all just start shouting each other's names and start going in for the hugs because we are excited to see people we love and want them to know it.

4 See people for who they are because we are all just humans.

When I am with my little five-year-old buddies, whether we're at home or out and about, I try to be really engaged with them. I want them to know how much I love them and want to build a relationship with them. So if you ever see me in public with them, you may see me doing an epic handshake with this little dude after a touchdown on his favorite football game on my phone or role-playing with this little beauty because she likes to "play Sadie" so she can use my lip gloss. Or I may be in the process of wiping off numerous boogers (they think the funniest thing in the world is to put them on me!).

Often when we are out, and sometimes in the middle of our game or silly little conversations, someone will interrupt to ask to take a photo with me. The look on the kids' faces is pure confusion. They do not understand why people would do this. They ask, "Why are they taking a picture with Sadie?"

> The truth is, we are all human.

Their little minds are on our game. Our conversations. They just see me as me, so why would someone who doesn't know me take a picture with me?

Sometimes I feel that in a world of celebrities and Instagram followings, people look at others with wider eyes the more followers they have. They treat you a little differently and look at you a whole lot differently than those they consider "regular people." The truth is, we are all human. Something I appreciate about my five-year-old friends is that they see all people as human. If you're nice and cool with boogers, then you are a friend. If you are mean and do not know how to laugh at yourself, you're probably not going to be their friend. These are good criteria. We are all just human. Be nice. Be willing to play and don't mind a booger or two from a friend.

5 Surround yourself with cheerleaders, for they will cheer you on to be the best version of yourself.

I have heard that by the time people are five years old, much of who they are is already programmed in them. This makes a lot of sense to me. When I was five, I got up on a table and started preaching to my parents. There is a video of it on YouTube because during my preaching as a five-year-old little girl, living in the woods of Calhoun, Louisiana, I said something very strange. I said, "Even if I am famous one day, I will not think about myself, but I am giving it to God."

Then I continued to sing a little jingle I had made up titled "Let's Give It Up for God," followed by "Woo-

> Fear has no authority over you.

hoo!" and an epic toe-touch. I preached the truth I knew, unafraid and unashamed. I was just simply in love with God, and I spoke a simple truth.

When *Duck Dynasty* started, people started asking me to speak publicly for the first time, and fear gripped me. I said no to most of the invitations. I put a lot of stress on myself trying to come up with a message. I feared what people thought. I wondered if I would have enough material to fill twenty minutes and if I was even quali-fied to be on a stage speaking. Somewhere along the way between the time I was five and my teenage years, I allowed other voices into my life—voices of self-doubt and lack of faith and trust in God. When I was five years old, I had confidently climbed up our family's coffee table (my stage) and spoken loudly and boldly about the truth I knew and the love I had for God. At that time, if they had given me a ten-minute timer, someone would have had to carry me off the stage still preaching. As a young adult, recapturing the confidence I had as a five-year-old took some time. I have it now, but finding it again was a process.

Recapture your confidence.

When my little buddies and I were playing worship leaders and they were singing at the top of their lungs about their love for God, I stopped for a minute to pray that their sense of freedom in worship would never end. I prayed that fear would have no authority over their lives to take away their worship, that words of shame would never be spoken over them to silence their voices—and that if the words of the world are spoken, they would raise their shields of faith to defend any arrow coming against them. I prayed that they would protect their ears and be careful about the voices they allow into their minds and that their worship would silence their enemies.

I believe that when we are five, the reason we are often and weirdly our best and most fun selves is partly because of our child-like manner. But I also think our confidence and freedom come from the voices around us and our parents' protection over who is allowed to speak into our lives. We hear voices of encouragement, voices of truth—voices telling us we are enough, telling us that we are beautiful just as we are, telling us how loved we are, telling us how to be strong when we feel weak or hurt, bringing out our originality, and disciplining us out of love.

But whether or not you had this growing up, there comes a point in life when we have to begin to do this for ourselves. We have to learn to guard our hearts, guard our ears, guard our eyes—and not allow the world to take away the things that really make us who we are. Because what makes us uniquely who we are is what makes us real and what empowers us to truly live.

Jesus "called a little child to him, and placed the child among them. And he said: 'Truly I tell you, unless you change and become like little children, you will never enter the kingdom of heaven. Therefore, whoever takes the lowly position of this child is the greatest in the kingdom of heaven'" (Matthew 18:2–4). Having a child's perspective helps us prioritize what God says is most important, so let's see the world through a five-year-old's eyes.

When you're a child, you know what you know, and you believe what you believe. As best as I can tell, it's the same when you're eighty-five. It seems to me that it's in the middle that people struggle, question, and argue about petty things.

It's nice to have five-year-old friends, and it's also nice to have an eighty-five-year-old friend. Mine is my great-grandmother, Mamaw Jo.

She keeps it real.

She keeps you real.

She keeps perspective real.

She keeps life real.

She is just real.

Interestingly, the five things I appreciate in my five-year-old friends are the same qualities I appreciate in Mamaw Jo. My five-year-old friends have been on earth only a few short years. Mamaw Jo was born in the 1930s—when Franklin Roosevelt was president of the United States, before World War II broke out, before Jeeps were invented, and before the first ballpoint pen was created. She's seen a lot—and learned a lot—during her lifetime, and some of it reminds me of how the five-year-olds see life. They're just looking forward at it, and she is looking backward. Funny, though, how in the middle, those years between five and eighty-five, we forget a lot of these things. Maybe they seem too simple or too childlike. But as Mamaw Jo has proven to me, they are the things that rise to the top when all the trappings of life fall to the ground—after so many years of living what my family and I believe to be a remarkable life.

Here are the things Mamaw Jo thinks are important.

1 Live in the moment.

Mamaw Jo remembers when entertainment was entertainment, when performers were dedicated to helping a crowd have fun, not to stroking their egos. When we go to concerts or events today, we become so busy filming them so we can post videos that we miss the entertainment of it. I know what Mamaw Jo would say about that: "Why are you filming this? You should be dancing!"

> Relax and enjoy the good times God gives us.

In her day, a well-known singer performed at her high school prom. He didn't do it for himself; he did it so they would be able to dance. His goal was to help them enjoy the moment and create great memories. That's all. That would never happen today!

I think we should try to relax and enjoy the good times God gives us instead of trying so hard to document them. Just as my five-year-old friend said, "We are not supposed to take pictures. We are just supposed to sing," Mamaw Jo would say, "You don't need to be filming everything. *You are just supposed to dance.*" She didn't even have a way to film people back then. But she's still sharing her memories of her prom today!

2 Surround yourself with laughter and the people you love, and your day will be a good one.

Mamaw Jo has a great sense of humor, and she loves to laugh.

When I was about five years old, I said to her, "You have a bump on your nose."

Immediately she responded, "Well, you have a bump on your face."

I didn't know what she was talking about, and I remember her chuckling as I tried to figure it out.

I finally realized the bump on my face was my nose. She thought that was funny, and so did I. It became our private little joke. She doesn't take herself too seriously, even though she is a highly respected person.

Mamaw Jo truly enjoys her life. She has a positive attitude, she's a happy person, and she laughs every chance she gets. She's built her life on faith and family, and when people do that, they can find something good in every day.

> If you build your life on faith and family, you'll find something good in every day.

3 Let people know how happy you are to see them. You may just make their day!

I'm thankful to say that there are a lot of things on earth I know I can count on. One of them is that Mamaw Jo will always be thrilled to see me. Every time we see each other, she gives me a big smile and a hug and says something like, "Hi, honey, it's *so wonderful* every time I get to see you!"

She never tries to make me feel bad because I don't see her as much as I used to. She's just happy when we do get to be together. The fact that she's always glad to see me makes me feel so special and so loved! I try to remember that I can make other people feel special, like she does for me, and you can too! It really is simple, and it goes a long way.

4 See people for who they are because we are all just humans.

Mamaw Jo probably gets the fact that we are all just humans better than anyone I know. No matter how the dynamics of my life have changed—and they have changed a *lot* over the past several years— the dynamics of my relationship with her have stayed the same. I admit it; my life has changed, and that has thrown some people off. But not Mamaw Jo. She sees me, knows me, and loves me for who I am. When I am home in Louisiana, I still have coffee with her and just talk as often as possible.

She's lived long enough to understand that no one is better than anybody else, that everyone struggles, that everyone has victories and things that make him or her happy. She knows there's nobody perfect except Jesus. She respects everyone and admires some people, but she doesn't idolize anyone. She can see people's faults and frailties, but she doesn't hold those things against them. She doesn't let anyone's attitude or response to her determine how she treats him or her; she's going to be kind anyway.

5 Surround yourself with cheerleaders, for they will cheer you on to be the best version of yourself.

The people in my family are my biggest encouragers and cheerleaders. Even though Mamaw Jo is the oldest of us all, she never lets that keep her from pulling for me. When I was younger, she attended school events and cheered me on from the stands during my basketball games. Now that I'm older, she has traveled to Fashion Week in New York City and to *Dancing with the Stars* to support me.

She even shows up on the Live Original tour, which is a traveling worship and speaking event that my team and I started in 2016.

She is a huge supporter of whatever I do. In fact, I cannot remember anything significant that

> It will give you life to "do life" with others.

I have done without her being part of it, down to making me a chocolate sheet cake almost every year for my birthday. I know she is always there for me, and I will always be grateful for that. As much as she does that for me, I also want to do that for others—to listen, care, support, and encourage them. It gives me life to "do life" with others around me.

I wanted to share these lessons from five-year-olds and an eighty-five-year-old to show that anyone can choose to live at any point. No matter what age or stage you find yourself in, you can show up for the day and show up for others.

Stretch for Your Song

WHAT GIVES YOU LIFE? WHAT STIRS UP YOUR PASSION AND energy? What do you love so much that you forget to eat when you're doing it? What makes time fly for you? What would you do if you never got paid to do it—or if you had to pay someone to let you do it? *That's* what makes your heart sing.

If you want to know how to really live, part of the answer is to find the song your heart wants to sing and sing it out with everything you have.

I like to sing, but I'm insecure when it comes to singing in front of an audience. I really do not know why it makes me so nervous, but it does. In her audiobook *This Is Me*, Chrissy Metz tells a story about a time someone asked her if she would ever do more music, and she laughed. She suddenly felt convicted for laughing because she realized that it doesn't make people feel good when you don't acknowledge the blessings you've been given.[11] Not feeling as though she would be good enough to pursue music made her laugh at someone who was trying to pay her a compliment. Man, have I been there. Not a good feeling. Resisting a compliment, in a way, is speaking death to yourself, while embracing it brings life.

After my first book, *Live Original*, came out and started to find a following, I realized more than ever how much people crave this message of positivity and hope in their lives. So we thought, *Why not go on tour?* An amazing team helped me pull together some incredible speakers, musicians, and leaders to visit sixteen cities around the United States and share with them God's encouragement and direction for our lives. So when the Live Original team and I were planning our 2018 tour, with the theme "United We Stand, Divided We Fall," I really wanted us to have a song or an anthem to go along with the tour so people could remember it. Even though this happened only about a month before the tour kicked off—which is *ridiculous* (getting a song recorded usually takes months, not a couple of weeks)—I got together with Leslie Jordan from the band All Sons and Daughters and with the great producer Hank Bentley, and we wrote a little anthem for the tour. It was simple, but it was powerful to sing with a crowd of people.

We need to stretch.

As the tour approached and we had this song we had written, a question arose: "Ummmm, who is going to lead this song, considering we do not have our own worship band?" Seriously, books need emojis because I really could use the crying laughing face here. They don't call our team "young and scrappy" for nothing!

I ended up saying I would do it, and next thing I knew, I was standing in a studio wearing headphones with a microphone in my

WHAT MAKES
YOUR HEART
SING?

face. Hank's patience with the number of questions I asked that day makes him a legend.

This will make music people squirm, but about an hour and a half into the recording, I'd been late or early on the timing *every single time*, and Hank asked me if I was hearing the clicks okay.

| There is
| a song
| in you.

(When you're singing to a track with head-phones on, soft clicks play in your ears to keep you on the beat.) My response was, "Oh, yes. They are driving me crazy! I've been trying to tune them out." For nonmusical people like me, the clicks are supposed to keep you on time, which explains my continued off-timing belt-outs. Truly, I knew *nothing* about recording studios. Eight hours went by that day, and by the end of it we were all exhausted.

Here is where it gets good. I asked Hank how many times it takes "normal" recording artists to get their songs, and he said it typically takes around eight to twenty times max.

I then gulped and prepared myself for my next question, "Okay, cool. So how many times did it take me?"

He responded, "Two hundred eleven."

We all busted out laughing. I told him I kind of felt like I just took 211 face-plants in front of everyone. He and my whole team laughed, but everyone in that room, along with me, wholeheartedly believed that this song was so much bigger than 211 face-plants.

Sure, there were some bad pitches and some bad timing here and there, but the song was to be an anthem for people to declare over themselves that they are a part of the family of God.

What's my point? It's okay to laugh at yourself as you do the things God has called you to do. Take some risks. Face-plant. Laugh about it. But it is not okay to bury the talents and gifts God has given you or to hold back because of fear.

TAKE SOME RISKS. FACE-PLANT. LAUGH ABOUT IT.

When situations like these come up in our lives, requiring us to do something we do not necessarily believe we are the best at, I like to just say we are "stretching." We are reaching for something that lies just beyond what is comfortable for us. Sometimes this happens in a moment, but other times we go through whole seasons of stretching. One definition of *stretch* is "to cause (someone) to make maximum use of their talents or abilities."[12] (And by the way, *stretch* is a verb, just like *live*. Just saying.) Even if that ability isn't so impressive yet, stretching yourself is the only way it will grow.

Before athletes take off to win a race, they have to stretch their muscles. They have to lean in to the uncomfortable tight places of their bodies, places that may be a little stiff and unworked, but that's the only way for them to function at their maximum potential. In a way, we're all athletes. We need to stretch. It's good for us, and it will prepare us to do, to the best of our ability, what we're created to do.

I believe there is a song in you. It may not be a literal song; it may be a dream, a vision, or a longing in your heart. It may be the opportunity to do what you love or a chance to invest your love in unusual ways. That's what your song is. As I mentioned earlier in the book, God has given you life so you can live and fulfill His unique purpose for you. He's made you an original, and your song is original too. He wants your heart to sing, but you may have to stretch for your song.

> Our capacity has to increase—or stretch—so God can give us more, show us more, teach us more, and use us more.

Throughout the Bible, God did amazing things through ordinary people, and most of those things were not easy or comfortable. God is not nearly as interested in making things comfortable for us as we would like Him to be. He requires us to stretch because He wants us to grow and become stronger. He wants to give us more than we have right now, but we are holding all we can hold with the capacity we currently have. Our capacity has to increase—or stretch—so God can give us more, show us more, teach us more, and use us more.

The people in the Bible stretched, and you can too. That's the only way you'll be able to sing your song and the only way the world will ever hear it.

Kill the Green-Eyed Monster

ONE DAY I WAS WATCHING *THE PRINCESS DIARIES* WITH one of my good friends, Emma Jenkins. During one scene in the movie, both of our jaws dropped. The fact that I was watching it with Emma is significant, as I will explain later.

In the movie, a seemingly ordinary high school girl named Mia, played by Anne Hathaway, finds out that she is a princess. This new-found royal title comes with a lot of attention Mia has never experienced before—a lot of drama, unwanted media attention, hate comments, and even distance and misunderstanding between her and her best friend, Lilly. Lilly is one of those young people who wants to change the world and does everything she knows to make that happen, including hosting her own cable television show. But she acts less than thrilled when her best friend suddenly becomes a princess.

The scene that caught our attention is when Lilly and Mia are talking on the school basketball court one day. Lilly is letting Mia have it, pouring out her heart—up until the point when Mia blurts out, "You got your wish! I am not going to be a princess!"

Suddenly, Lilly's tone completely changes. She becomes sad and says, "You're not?"

What Lilly says next surprises Mia and might surprise you too. Lilly says, "But I want you to be."

Mia makes the most exhausted and completely confused face and simply says, "What?"

Lilly says that she hasn't really meant any of the negative comments she has made about the big changes in Mia's life. She said them, she confesses, because "the green monster of jealousy came out" when Mia became "Miss Popular."

Then Lilly speaks one of my favorite lines in the movie: "I told you: *I need an attitude adjustment!* But the truth is, you being a princess is kind of a miracle."

Mia responds, "What! No! What miracle? It's a nightmare!"

Mia is overwhelmed with all the unwanted drama, division between her and her best friend, and unsolicited commentary from seemingly everyone in the world.

But Lilly responds, "I just found out that my cable show only reaches twelve people. Wanting to rock the world but having zip power like me, now *that* is a nightmare. But you, wow."

Mia responds, still a little confused, "What is so wow?"

Then Lilly speaks the most incredible words in the most nonchalant way: "'Wow' is having the power to effect change. . . . What more of a miracle do you want?"[13]

FOCUS ON
ALL THE
GOOD IN
YOUR LIFE.

When we heard those words, Emma and I let out our own "Wow."

The power to effect change *is* a miracle.

Emma Jenkins has been a good friend all my life. She is one of the kindest and most encouraging humans I have ever met. She overflows with the fruit of who Jesus is and has more Scripture memorized and deeply rooted in her than anyone I know. Her sweet spirit and encouraging messages on Instagram, YouTube,

> The power to effect change *is* a miracle.

and her blogs have gained her quite the following. I understand firsthand what can come with having a following—both the great things and the not-so-great things—so I had invited Emma to come and stay with me for a couple of days to encourage her and speak truth in whatever way I could.

While Emma was with me, news spread that a famous YouTube creator had put out a roast video about her. I watched Emma as she just kept smiling and quoting scriptures that warn of such things happening. Then she carried on with her day. Her family called and told her not to watch it and reminded her of truth. I don't know why the YouTube creator chose to roast her, but I do know that she chose to respond with amazing strength, maturity, and grace.

Once in an interview on a red carpet, someone asked me if I fear that I will go wild like other celebrities who started as Christians do.

I said, "No, I do not fear that, but I can certainly see how it can happen."

I meant that. I can totally see how some celebrities can walk away from their faith—or seem to turn their backs on it. Because when your life is suddenly in the spotlight and you stand for faith, the secular world mocks you. On top of that, the church world can tend to be uber-critical of you, and jealousy creeps into your friendships. It's easy to start believing what people who don't even know you say about you instead of what you know to be true about yourself. If you let those things discourage you, I can see how you could get to the point Princess Mia reached and just say, "Okay, fine! You got your wish. I am not going to be a princess anymore!"

Something like what happened to Mia in *The Princess Diaries* happens to many of us when we start really living—when we start living with more confidence and boldness, when we begin doing things that others are too scared to do, when we start speaking words of life and truth. Our lives begin to look different, and jealousy rears its ugly head.

My family describes it like this: "If you're carrying the football, you're going to get tackled." Sometimes we want to just put the football down so we won't get tackled, but that is not the life God invites us to live.

Think of how many voices have been silenced. I wonder how many times hope has been snuffed out because of jealousy from the world or, even worse, within the church.

Let me add that this kind of jealousy is not a twenty-first-century celebrity problem. And it's not just celebrities. When *any* person does something or has something another one wants, feelings of envy get stirred up. The green-eyed monster has been around since Bible times.

Let's look at the book of Acts, when the church was just getting started. Notice that every time a crowd formed, so did jealousy.

In Acts 5:12, the apostles were healing many people. Such a powerful wave of healing was happening that people were bringing the sick into the streets and laying them on beds and mats. People did not even have to be touched to be healed. They were healed just because Peter's shadow fell on them as he passed by.

CHERISH WHAT MAKES

YOU DIFFERENT.

Crowds of people were there to be healed—and all of them were. That's something to celebrate! But Acts 5:17-18 says that "the high priest and all his associates, who were member of the party of the Sadducees, were filled with jealousy. They arrested the apostles and put them in the public jail." What a heartbreak.

In Acts 13, Paul and Barnabas had just finished speaking in the synagogue. Verse 43 of that chapter says that many of the Jews and devout converts to Judaism followed Paul and Barnabas, who talked with them and urged them to continue in the grace of God! Yet here they go again: "When the Jews saw the crowds, they were filled with *jealousy*. They began to contradict what Paul was saying and heaped abuse on him" (Acts 13:45).

The people eventually kicked Paul and Barnabas out of the region. Acts 13:51-52 says that they "shook the dust off their feet [which is something Jesus commands in Matthew 10:14 and Luke 9:5 when people will not receive those who are doing God's work] . . . and went to Iconium. And the disciples were filled with joy and with the Holy Spirit." Again, they were shut down and Paul and Barnabas were forced to leave because of what? Jealousy!

Then, believe it or not, the same thing happened again. Acts 17 says that as Paul and Silas were preaching to a group of people about Jesus, Jews, many God-fearing Greeks, and quite a few prominent women were persuaded to believe! Look at what happens right after this, according to Acts 17:5: "But other Jews were *jealous*; so they rounded up some bad characters from the marketplace, formed a mob and started a riot in the city. They rushed to Jason's house in search of Paul and Silas in order to bring them out to the crowd." Yet another amazing move of God was stopped by jealousy.

Proverbs 27:4 says, "Anger is cruel and fury overwhelming, but who can stand before jealousy?" Standing against jealousy and its impact is hard, but it is possible.

If you have ever felt the sting of jealousy as Peter and the apostles, Paul, Barnabas, and Silas did, simply follow Paul and Barnabas's example: shake the dirt off your feet and walk on with joy, knowing the Holy Spirit is with you. You did all you could do with the best intentions, so just keep going.

If, however, you are the one feeling jealous and lashing out at others, realize that it's a miserable feeling that comes from a place of deep hurt. Start reading scriptures that will help you heal, talk to a counselor or trusted friend (just make sure you approach someone mature who isn't jealous of the same person!), and deal with the pain so you can enjoy the good things God is doing. Living in jealousy will cause you to miss out on some amazing moments—or cause others to miss them!

> Living in jealousy will cause you to miss out on some amazing moments.

Some situations make you wonder, *How could I not be jealous?* Well, you can *choose* not to be jealous because you can resist the temptation to compare yourself with other people. If you focus on all the good in your life—instead of what you envy about someone else—jealousy can't stand.

Often the root of jealousy is that we think someone is cool and we're not or that other people get to do cool things and we don't. I like to say, "Cool is what you make it."

Cool is not a certain look or a certain way of acting or liking the "right" things and disliking the nerdy ones. It's just being confident in what you're doing and in who you are.

One time I wore a blazer that was quite different from what

other people around me were wearing at the time. And I could not stop dancing when I put it on. I thought it was cool, and I felt good in it—and that's what mattered. I remembered that I used to compare myself to everyone around me. I wanted to make sure my clothes were like theirs and to make sure our makeup looked similar and our legs were similar sizes. So much similar! That is exhausting and impossible!

God didn't make us all the same for a reason. He did it intentionally, and that's cool to me. Look around: no one is just like you! Cherish what makes you different from every other person in the world.

Here's my challenge:

Stop comparing your legs to the person beside you, and just compare your left to your right and use them to their best potential. Stop waiting to see what all your friends are wearing and just wear what you *love* because you love it! Stop making sure your makeup is on trend and just do it the way that makes you feel confident, and if you do not like to wear makeup, then don't. When you become confident, you become cool with who you are. And when you're cool with who you are, you won't be jealous of anything or anyone around you.

In *The Princess Diaries*, Lilly's anger really comes from her belief that she is losing her best friend. That is painful and scary to her. And sometimes we feel the same way. When someone else is being seen and heard, we can be afraid

> Cool is being confident in what you're doing and in who you are.

we are "losing" someone or something that matters to us.

But others' successes don't take anything away from us. There isn't a limited supply of success out there. For example, in the church, if someone is preaching the name of Jesus, it's good for all of us. The fact that God chooses to elevate or shine a spotlight on one person for a season does not steal from your own purpose. It only benefits it!

In the movie, Lilly is influencing the lives of twelve people on her cable show, and Mia has the opportunity to influence a whole country. But Lilly misses the fact that they both have an opportunity to effect change. Mia's rise to fame is only going to help Lilly's show too.

> Let's cheer each other on. Let's help each other succeed.

I played basketball throughout high school, and I remember seeing two people on our own team fighting over the ball. When that happened, everyone else on the team would yell, "Same team!" because we could see that if one of them had the ball, then our team had an advantage.

This is how we need to see life. Let's cheer each other on. Let's help each other succeed. Let's not ever fight over the ball with someone on our own team.

Being who you are as a child of God is a miracle, and it comes with miraculous power through the help of the Holy Spirit! Your testimony and your prayers have the power to effect change no matter how many people follow you.

Let me encourage you: do not be discouraged if you have only twelve people listening, and do not be discouraged if you have twelve million listening and many of them make hurtful comments. Live the life God calls you to live, and don't worry about the rest.

There's More to Come

A FEW YEARS AGO, I HIT A LOW POINT. A *REALLY* LOW POINT. It was the week my book *Live Fearless* came out, to be exact, which is to pretty ironic. I was coming out of a brief but tough relationship that ended up hurting my heart pretty badly. I was driving home after having a lot of hard conversations, and it was all weighing on me more heavily than it should have.

I struggle with not letting everyone know how I feel, because I do not want people to be sad or burdened by me. That night, and in the days leading up to it, I had been hiding the depth of the pain I was feeling from everyone close to me. That only made it harder to bear because I felt that the only place I could be fully human and cry was in the car. I knew that when I reached my next destination or had my next conversation, I would just laugh it off quickly; say, "All is well"; and continue telling myself I could deal with it.

That night I *had* to get back home because the next morning I was leaving for New York to do two full days of press for *Live Fearless*. I tend to think I am a pro at pulling myself together, but this time I really did not know how I could do that.

That's when I had the most terrible thought—a thought I struggle to even type out because I hate that my mind would even think something so depressing and negative. But after talking about this moment to several friends and hearing them say they have had similar thoughts, I want to be real about the place our minds can take us when we are hiding and running to the point of deep exhaustion—even people who seem the happiest.

I actually thought, *If I had a wreck right now, I do not think I would mind. I need a hard break no matter how I get it.* I didn't really mean that. I didn't want to end my life, but somehow in that moment, a month in the hospital in a body cast with other people taking care of me didn't seem so bad.

I want to say that I have such wonderful family and friends and an amazing team around me that had I simply said, "I need a break," everyone would have rallied around me. That could have easily happened, but the combination of secret pain and pride in my ability to pull it together led me to a dark, irrational thought instead of being honest about how I was feeling.

That night, right after my mind "went there," within a split second I caught a glimpse of the moon. It was huge that night, one of those moons in which every detail seems magnified. Now, as weird as this may seem, when I was young, I used to think the moon was the earth. For real. Do not ask me how I managed to think

> One day does not define your life.

that logic was accurate, but I was convinced of it. I truly thought that when people on television showed pictures of earth, they were simply images of the moon with the blue and green coloring added. How I thought we were standing on the earth and could see all its roundness, I cannot explain. I don't know what I was thinking. I would look up and think, *Wow. It's a big world.* In my little brain I just thought it was the coolest thing to look up and see the earth.

Against the dark sky that night, in an instant, I caught a glimpse of the moon, and I sensed the Lord saying, *Sadie, this world is a lot bigger than you. If you want to quit because you think your problems are too great to handle, then you will lead many others to do the same.*

You might be in a similar place, but please know that you're worth a lot more than your feelings will tell you. On any given day, things may get chaotic for you. You may be super stressed and really want to take a break from everything. But it's so important to remember that one day—no matter how rough it is—does not define the rest of your life. Your purpose and calling give you an important place in the world. Do not give up. There is so much more to come.

By now you know that I really like *The Princess Diaries*, and I want to mention another scene from it that captures this perfectly. In that scene, Princess Mia feels completely overwhelmed and wants to give up, but her security guard, Joe, says, "No one can quit being who they really are, not even a princess. Now you can refuse the job, but you are a princess by birth."

Princess Mia responds, "How can I tell if I can even do the job?"

And Joe replies, "By simply, simply trying."[14]

Many times we want to be sure we can do something before we even try. The thought that we might not succeed makes us nervous

YOU'RE
WORTH A LOT
MORE THAN
YOUR FEELINGS
WILL TELL YOU.

about making the effort. We may hesitate because we feel we are not smart enough, pretty enough, or popular enough, or because we don't think we have the time or energy to fully commit to it. For some reason, we don't feel we can fulfill what the opportunity will require of us, and then we don't feel good about ourselves.

I once spoke at an event where all the girls in the room were asked to write about who they thought they were. Each one had a sheet of paper that said at the top, "I am [blank]," and they were to fill in the blank. I noticed that all the girls were using adjectives that were rather negative to describe their identity. Then I realized that adjectives are used to describe how people may feel, but they are not used to describe the essence of who a person is.

> Only God can truly define you.

I have seen and heard many people say they believe that they are worthless. That is a scary lie to identify with because believing it never leads to anything good. Feelings of worthlessness begin to creep in when we feel we cannot fulfill what is being asked of us. Then we want to give up because we are overwhelmed.

For Princess Mia, the position into which she was born felt like too much. She didn't think she could ever measure up to it. But if you've seen the whole movie, you know that she could. She needed the right training and wisdom from those more experienced, and she needed the courage to take some good advice. Regardless of the way she felt, the truth is that the whole story is not about what she had to offer but about who she was. No matter what other factors were involved, she was royalty because she was born into it.

I wonder about you. Have you ever been in a position where you said to yourself, "I can't do this" or "I won't get this right" or "This is too much for me"? Maybe you need to hear what Mia heard and eventually came to believe: you're royalty. And that's not because of what you can do.

Mia's comments about feeling inadequate took place after she had already received a nice makeover, a sleek new hairstyle, and lessons on how to walk like a lady in heels. Outwardly, she looked like a royal, but it wasn't about her look. Change happened for her when she decided to fulfill what she was born to fulfill. It's that whole "know to realize" thing, remember?

In life, you will face all kinds of situations in which the world will try to tell you who you are. People may say that you are not very smart or that you are awkward or that you "have issues" or that your dreams will never come true or that you are worth nothing because of where you came from, who your parents are, the house you live in, the color of your skin, or where you buy your clothes. I beg you: don't let the world tell you who you are. Only God can truly define you. You can find out who you truly are by digging into His Word. And one thing you'll find there is that you are royalty. You are a child of the King of the universe. You don't have to be overwhelmed by anything or intimidated by anyone. You're God's royal son or daughter, which means you can do whatever He calls you to do. All you have to do is try, and He will do the rest.

Read this and take it personally: you are far from worthless.

I know that a lot of young people do feel worthless, though, so I want to address it a bit more. Ephesians 5:11 says, "Have nothing to do with the fruitless deeds of darkness, but rather expose them." What I believe tends to happen, just like what was happening to me that night on my drive home, is that you begin to soak in hidden, fruitless lies in the darkness of your heart. You replay the hard conversations you have had and the most painful moments you

> You are far from worthless.

have been through, the ones that caused shame to rise up in you. Instead of exposing those fruitless thoughts, you let them lead you to believe that you are worthless. I repeat: *you* are not worthless, but the lies and the adjectives you are believing about yourself are *worth less* than the identity of royalty God has on your life as a son or a daughter of the King.

It really does not matter what season of life you are in or even if you are simply having a bad day that makes you feel negative about yourself. You will always be royalty, and you will always be loved— you can never quit who you are, because these truths are already established. It's time to reject the lies of the Enemy and embrace the royalty that God has given you.

You can refuse the job of royalty, so to speak, by never exposing the fruitless and worthless thoughts in your head to the light. If you continue to believe the lies, it's as if you've quit being a prince or princess. But to take on your royal role, you simply need to see the truth of who you are and redeem your view of the world around you. When the Enemy can get you to set your focus on your own problems, it is easy to think that what you do and believe about your-self affects only you. But when you catch a glimpse of the world around you and are reminded of the

> The King of the universe created you.

worth in you, then you can truly see that your decision to just try can have a massive impact on those around you.

On the night the moon was so big and bright, I am glad I did not try my usual pull-it-together mentality to somehow pack late at night and then wake up the next morning for the earliest flight out of Nashville to New York to talk for hours in front of a camera about living fearless. At that time, my strength was exhausted, and my mind-set would have made it impossible for me to get the job done in a worthy way. But when God spoke that night, it led me into a lot of prayer, and when I called a good friend and let her in on exactly where my heart was, it exposed all the dark and fruitless things I'd been thinking and brought them into the light.

I woke up the next day with a totally new perspective, passion, and God-given strength to take my trip. *Live Fearless* released and became a bestseller on Amazon the very next day, allowing me to share with millions of people my testimony of how my faith in God overcame my fears. Thank God I didn't quit because of my own little perspective. Thank God He reminded me that I am royalty. I belong to Him. He enabled me to do what I needed to do that day and to overcome the negativity of the day before. Because I spoke so much about *Live Fearless*, and because it is a message He has blessed, many people have found freedom from fear and experienced a new level of freedom and confidence in God they never knew was possible. I like to think they are realizing that they are royalty too!

Have you ever thought about the fact that you are royalty? The King of the universe created you, which makes you—yes, you—a child of the King. *That's* your worth. You cannot quit being royal, because that's what you have always been—even before you were born, when the King of the world knit you together in your mother's womb (Psalm 139:13). Now, what you choose to do with your position as a child of the King is totally up to you. How you step into it, how you receive it, and what you even believe about it is in your hands.

Throw
Yourself a
Dance Party

MY FRIEND AND I WERE DANCING DOWN AN AISLE IN Walmart one day, and a seventy-six-year-old woman named Mrs. Elma came up laughing and said, "I just had so much fun watching you have fun in life. Not many people do that anymore. I have always told myself not to care what people think and to have fun, no matter what. If I want to dance in a store, I will dance. If I want to skip down a street, I will skip. Keep skipping through life, girls, and God bless."

I seriously believe that dancing is a universal language of freedom. On one of my trips to Haiti, I was walking with a group around the streets to support some local business owners who had just graduated from a program we were working with. As we were walking, a group of children began to follow us. In our group, no one spoke a single word of Creole, and none of them spoke a word of English, but we wanted to communicate with the children. Since I had nothing to say, I just busted out some classic dance moves and then pointed at them. They laughed and repeated what I did. We ended up sharing dance moves back and forth for probably an hour and created great memories without ever saying a word.

Dancing is also a universal invitation. It enables people to become part of each other's lives because it brings people together. It is lively and expressive, and it can communicate all by itself. I have been in the most random circles with people who speak different languages, believe different things, and have completely different life stories, yet we were still able to have an amazing time together by breaking it down on the dance floor. Just think about a wedding reception: all kinds of people come together because they are some-how connected to the ones getting married. And they can celebrate with each other in a fun way by dancing. I've personally seen dance break the ice and bond large groups of people with little in common faster than any words I could have said.

I want to give you a glimpse into three stories about times when dancing has formed a bond between me and some people I first thought were very unlikely dance partners!

1 Private Christian School

I was sharing a message at a high school girls' Bible study. The girls were all seniors at a private Christian school, and when I walked in and read the room, I could tell they were going to be a tough crowd. We all know how high school girls can be and the intimidat-ing stares they can give—stares that go straight to the soul to see if you will rise or fall while they are watching you. Okay, maybe that is too dramatic, but so are high school girls, so it feels necessary.

DANCING IS A UNIVERSAL

LANGUAGE OF FREEDOM.

I got out my Bible that day and talked for a minute, but in the face of their stares and blank expressions, I simply said, "Man! Y'all are intimidating! And you know, as daughters of the King, we are not supposed to live lives that intimidate but that invite people in."

I could tell I was not making much progress with them, so I took a huge risk and said, "You know what we are going to do? I already know that at first it is going to be awkward as all get out, but we are going to *dance*!"

They gave me room full of cold stares, and I could pretty much hear through their eyes, *Noooooooo!*

But I continued, "I'm going to dance as long as I have to and as long as you stare at me—until everyone in this room is dancing with me."

I turned on the song "Not Today Satan" and started dancing. And yes, it was extremely awkward at first, but after about two minutes every girl was dancing—the quiet ones, the loud ones, the popular ones, the awkward ones, the athletes, the artists—all of them were dancing together. And I watched as tiny high school cliques formed one big bond.

I later found out that that dance party broke down many walls for that senior class and that they made T-shirts for every girl in the class with an inside joke from the dance party. They even joked about it from the stage at their graduation, which I attended. They ended the school year differently than they started it because they let go of trying to intimidate with their glares and stances and learned to express themselves as free and fun, doing something that invited everyone in!

2 Juvenile Detention

Earlier in this book, I wrote about teaching a Bible study at juvie. The first time I went was because I heard that a local church was going to do ministry work with the girls, and I decided I wanted to go with them. I did not even know what church I was going with, nor did I know anyone in the ministry group. I certainly was not planning on teaching, speaking, or doing anything that would cause me to stand out or be visible to the girls in detention. I just knew I wanted to go to juvie.

When we arrived, I tagged along behind the team and watched what they did from afar. When the girls walked into the room where we were waiting for them, I felt instantly intimidated! If you know much about me, you know that the more intimidated I feel, the more awkward I get. So that day, I reverted to a lesson from the movie *Madagascar*: "Just smile and wave, boys. Smile and wave."[15]

> Love bridges the gap between people.

I'm pretty sure no one smiled and waved back.

The leader of our group asked the girls to be seated, and someone began teaching. I simply observed the situation, kind of feeling sorry for the teacher because no one in the audience seemed at all interested in what she had to say.

Then our group leader walked over to me and said something I had never heard before, but it turned out to be one of the greatest things ever. She said, "You have the anointing of a dance party!"

I didn't even know there *was* an anointing for a dance party!

I laughed and thought, *That's hilarious.*

Then she said, "Okay, get it started!"

I looked at her like she was crazy. Then I looked at the girls from juvie, sitting in front of me with their blank stares at best and downright angry expressions at worst. I looked back at the leader and said, "Ummmm, are you serious?"

She said, "Yes, look at your shirt! It's meant to be!"

I looked down, and sure enough I was wearing a shirt that read Dance Party. I wasn't sure if the whole "anointing for a dance party" was a word from God or just a message on my shirt.

She then took the microphone and said, "Girls, this is Sadie, and she is going to start a dance party."

I was so shocked that I needed a little time to take in what was happening and build up my courage to lead the dance party. Sometimes, when I get nervous, I fake a British accent just for fun.

"Hellooo," I said, "I'm going to d-ah-nce now."

I continued stalling, randomly throwing out words and fanning myself.

My next thought was, *Wait a minute. I have been in a place just like this before. These are just girls—just like the ones I talked to at the Bible study several months ago, so I might as well go for it.*

So I told them straight up, "Y'all are intimidating; I am not going to lie about that. But here is the thing. We are all just daughters, which makes us sisters. Sisters are not supposed to *intimidate* each other but to *invite* each other. We aren't supposed to try to make our sisters feel uncomfortable or less-than; we're supposed to invite them into our space and help them feel like they belong. If I walked into my sister's room at our home in Louisiana, I would be totally comfortable and at ease. I'd probably go in there dancing, smiling, laughing, and happy, knowing I was welcome. I don't know what y'all like to do with your sisters and your friends, but I like to dance!"

> We're supposed to invite people into our space and help them feel like they belong.

They began to smile and even to laugh a little. Now, if you are any kind of an entertainer, as I am, you know that a smile and a laugh can take you a long way. That's enough to get you to take the next step. Just a chuckle means full-send, baby. So I went for it.

Before I share any more about the dance party, let me say this: in life, to get to your anointing, you have to get past the awkwardness you feel and the awkward looks people give you. In case you're wondering, your "anointing" is whatever God has called, gifted, and empowered you to do.

I proceeded to do the weirdest dances I could think of. Once again, at first it was incredibly awkward. But then I began to see a few smiles and hear a few giggles.

Then one of the girls asked, "Sadie, do you know how to do the bunny hop?"

I didn't, so some of the girls got up and turned the song on using my phone and taught me the dance. By the end of the song, every single girl in juvie was doing the bunny hop dance together, smiling and laughing.

3 Live Original Tour Pizza Party

At a Live Original tour pizza party one night, a middle school girl was struggling to dance to the beat of the songs that were playing. I watched her from afar as she tried to join the crowd but grew more and more frustrated with herself.

She ran over to me and said, "Sadie, will you dance with me?"

Of course, I said yes!

She then broke into the weirdest and craziest dance moves I have ever seen, and I watched people around us start laughing. As I read the room and looked at this quiet girl becoming so confident in her moves, realizing people were laughing—at her, not with her—I joined her in the weirdest and craziest moves I could do.

We had so much fun! Then she stopped and stared at me being weird and crazy and motioned for me to lean in. She whispered, "You are my favorite person."

Pretty soon, everyone in the room had accepted her, and we were all dancing to "Footloose" together. I genuinely did not care what one other girl in the room thought of me that night. As long as that sweet girl knew she was a part of the group, I was going to dance with her, and it was going to be fun. That was a sister bond. Love bridges the gap between people.

> Be a part of the life in the room.

We're supposed to invite people into our space and help them feel like they belong.

Sometimes you will be the one who needs to start the dance party, and sometimes you will be the one who needs to join it. I wrote about starting two of them, and the outcome was amazing. I also joined one, and that was amazing too. Whatever part you play, just do it with all your heart. Be a part of the life in the room.

No matter how awkward you may feel bringing life to a dead room, dance until you see life rise up. Unite instead of divide. Welcome instead of intimidate. Don't give up because of a blank stare. An elderly lady in Walmart, a group of children from Haiti, seniors in a private Christian school, girls in juvie, and a middle school girl were able to acknowledge the family that we are because they were willing to share the freedom offered to all of us.

One, Two, Jump!

I HOPE YOU'VE HAD A CHANCE TO READ MY BOOK *LIVE Fearless* and that you are walking in more and more freedom over fear every day. As a result of my journey through fear, I decided that fear had been writing the story of my life for too long. So I started doing some things that once made me afraid, and I did them on purpose. On June 7, 2018, I jumped out of an airplane that was going 140 miles per hour at 14,000 feet above the ground.

Let me explain.

In the days leading up to this, whenever I felt fear, I quit running away from what frightened me and ran straight into it instead—as fast as I could. Every time I did this, boldness rose up in me. After running into so many scary situations recently and learning how to have peace through them, I asked myself, "What could I do to slap fear in the face?" Immediately I thought of skydiving.

As you read this story, don't think I'm encouraging you to skydive or to take a foolish risk. What I'm talking about is facing a fear. Your fear may be saying hello to someone you would like to have as a new friend or deciding to pay your way through college so you can get a degree. Maybe you have a fear of never losing weight, so you join a gym, or you have a fear of always being in debt like others in your family have been, so you hire a financial advisor. Whatever your fear is, I'm pretty sure you can identify it. And when you do, find a way to face it. It may be a lot less dramatic than my jumping out of a plane, but it's just as important.

My emotions were screaming, "No way!" But my heart was saying, "I can do all things through Christ who strengthens me" (Philippians 4:13 NKJV). I had learned that choosing to do something that pushes me or gets me out of my comfort zone when I don't have to is powerful and that God has placed the best things in life on the other side of fear. So I decided to go for it and made the arrangements.

When I woke up that morning, knowing I was going to do the scariest thing life could offer that day, I cannot tell you how insanely happy and excited I was. The whole idea of doing something so bold and adventurous put extra pep in my step. Even the people at my local coffee shop noticed a difference in me that morning and asked me why I was so awake and happy-go-lucky at 7:00 in the morning.

I noticed every single detail that morning about the people and the things around me. I even bought my coffee shop's logo laptop sticker, which I had seen every single day on the counter, just because—why not? The most remarkable thing about that morning was that I didn't have any fear at all. I felt alive—truly living life in the most epic freedom I've ever experienced.

When I arrived at the skydiving place, I started seeing familiar faces: a couple of friends, my mom, my sister-in-law Mary Kate, my sister Rebecca.

The next thing I knew, my mom said, "I'm jumping with you."

I still get emotional when I think about it. It was the most overwhelming act of love to have her standing with me (actually *jumping* with me).

If you read *Live Fearless*, you may know that my mom was there for me for every step of my journey as I battled to defeat fear. She calmed me when I was panicked and encouraged me when I was afraid. On skydiving day, she got to laugh with me and celebrate with me as I declared my freedom over fear in a new way. We were able to

> Fear taunts us and tries to intimidate us.

do something fun together, something we never could have done had it not been for my mom helping me put fear in perspective and go after freedom and for Jesus, who made it possible.

After my mom said she was jumping with me, my friends said, "Your *mom's* jumping with you? Then we're jumping too!"

We got suited up and listened to a brief tutorial about skydiving because, frankly, there isn't much to jumping out of a plane—not nearly as much as you might think or as there probably should be! We then walked awkwardly to the people who would be taking us on the dive. As we got strapped to them, I thought, *These are total strangers, and we are literally trusting them with our lives.*

As the plane took off, the guys who worked at the skydiving place started trying to scare us, making jokes about what could happen if the chute didn't open.

Those guys were simply teasing us, but when I thought about it later, I realized that they were doing exactly what fear does. Fear taunts us and tries to intimidate us. But when our hearts are established in the freedom God has given us, then we can laugh at the fear of the future.

No matter how the skydiving guys teased me, I was still able to step into a worship-filled moment, sensing God's presence. He was symbolically teaching me that I could let go of the control I wanted to exercise over my life and give up everything to Him. The old me would have been a slave to fear. I never would have let the idea of jumping out of a plane enter my mind. But God has given me—and He offers everyone—boldness and confidence in Him.

> You can be content even when you are not comfortable.

As the plane climbed upward, I had the most joyful peace I have ever felt. I kept saying, "Only in You, Jesus. This is something I can do only because of the freedom You have given me over fear."

This is what I was learning that day: in a life of faith, you are not always going to be comfortable. In fact, most acts of faith are not comfortable ones to take, but you can always be content. The definition of *comfort* is "a state of physical ease and freedom from pain or constraint."[16] The definition of *content* is "a state of peaceful happiness."[17] You can be content even when you are not comfortable. Hold on to that because it might get you to the next part of the story of your own life.

In the plane I scooted and inched my way toward the edge of the opening with this professional sky-diver awkwardly fastened to me by a hook that seemed way too small and looked as though it could easily pop off. I got up to the very edge, and judging by the video the company took of our jump, all ten of my chins were saying, "Noooo!" but my spirit was saying, "Yesssss!"

Soaring through the air was the wildest thing I have ever felt. Will Smith

described it perfectly in the YouTube video "What Skydiving Taught Me About Fear" when he said it is as if you're looking at death, but in a matter of seconds it's the most blissful experience you have ever felt.[18] I totally agree! It was a rush like no other—diving through the sky, higher than the birds and passing through the clouds. For the first ten seconds or so, it felt like chaos. Then I caught the wind.

Isn't it crazy that something perceived to be one of the most frightening things anyone can do was the most freeing experience I have ever had? It was exhilarating. It was fast and crazy. It was bold.

The moment that the chute was pulled, I screamed, "Why would I ever be afraid? God, You have me!" Then came a lot of *"Wow. Whoa. Amazing."*

After the moment when you pull the chute, your legs don't feel attached to your body anymore. You instantly become weightless, and suddenly, you're floating above earth. Really, though, you are floating above fear. For me, it was a moment of living fully alive.

I remember every moment of June 7, 2018, and just about every feeling I had and every facial expression of those around me. I still have my coffee shop sticker on my laptop, and I smile just remembering that morning before the jump.

Living fully alive means not letting fear keep you from experiencing the fullness of freedom. Your jump will not always be from an airplane in the sky. Your jump may look like a move to a new city, the first day of a new job, the start of a relationship, or anything that requires the uncontrol of the unknown. It is not missing a moment because of the uncomfortable hesitation fear causes or because of the fear of doing something alone. It is fully going for it all, whatever "it all" may be for you. It is letting go of control of the outcome and trusting people where they are and with the gifts they have. It's a whole lot of things, to be honest, and just a way to start really living.

> Don't let fear have the final say in your life.

My encouragement to you is this: don't let fear have the final say in your life. Don't even give it a vote. Don't let it make your decisions or steal your adventure with Jesus. As Will Smith said, "God has placed the best things in life on the other side of fear."[19] *And He's got you.*

Don't Waste the Waiting: Part 1

ONE DAY I WAS SITTING IN A COFFEE SHOP, MINDING MY own business, talking with my best friend and enjoying a coconut latte, my favorite in the whole world.

A guy who looked to be in his twenties came up to our table and wanted to talk to me. This happens fairly often because people know me from my family's television show, *Duck Dynasty*, they follow me on social media, or they've seen me speak somewhere, so I'm pretty used to it. But I never know what people are going to say, and sometimes their questions and comments are pretty interesting.

He said he wanted to ask me something, but he did *not* want me to give him the same answer his pastors and friends had given him. No pressure, right? All I could do was my best, and I was curious to find out what he wanted to talk about.

He opened up to us. "I am super frustrated with God," he said. "I grew up in a Christian family, and I did everything right. I followed all the rules, and I did my best to walk with God. But my brothers and sisters didn't. They did whatever they wanted to, and they didn't even try to follow the rules. Then they were accepted at the colleges where they wanted to go, and now they have the jobs they always wished for. They are thriving, and I am not. I didn't get into the college I wanted to go to. I don't have the job I want. Every time I ask someone why things have turned out this way for me, they say, 'You are just in a season of waiting.'"

I could tell he was growing more frustrated simply talking about his situation. "What does that mean?" he asked. "A season of waiting?"

It's something I've thought a lot about since this conversation, but let's first address the words he spoke prior to his final question. He was not simply frustrated with the fact that he was having to wait; he was angry that everyone else seemed to be getting what he believed he deserved. Do you ever feel this way? In today's world where we know everybody's business, how easy is it for us to see what our friends are doing or receiving and think, *Why am I over here having to wait? Why don't I have the dream job or my soul mate or the chance to travel the world?* Or maybe it's even as simple as this: *Why can't I afford those new shoes everyone is wearing?* Anybody spot the green-eyed monster? The killer duo—comparison and jealousy—rears its ugly head in the asking of these questions.

> When you are a child of God, you live in His house.

THERE ARE

LESSONS IN

THE WAITING.

Do you remember the prodigal son story we talked about earlier? Well, there is even more to that story. After the son returns from his wild living, the father throws him this amazing party, but his older brother is having none of it. Luke 15:28–32 says this:

> The older brother became angry and refused to go in. So his father went out and pleaded with him. But he answered his father, "Look! All these years I've been slaving for you and never disobeyed your orders. Yet you never gave me even a young goat so I could celebrate with my friends. But when this son of yours who has squandered your property with prostitutes comes home, you kill the fattened calf for him!"
>
> "My son," the father said, "you are always with me, and everything I have is yours. But we had to celebrate and be glad, because this brother of yours was dead and is alive again; he was lost and is found."

What an important reminder: when you are a child of God, you live in His house. He is with you always, even in the waiting.

The guy in the coffee shop had said he didn't want to be told he was in a season of waiting, but unfortunately, I didn't have any other answer. All those other people were right: he was having to wait. Being a child of God and doing "everything right" doesn't stop us from having to wait on things during this lifetime. There are lessons in the waiting and life to be lived.

You may have been there before. I definitely have. I think we all have. And sometimes, when we're in it, all we can think about is getting out of it, and we tend to waste the waiting. We could make the most of it, but instead we try to wish it away.

When God has us in a waiting season, there is so much we could be doing and so much He is working on. Sometimes we miss that, though, because we're so frustrated about the fact that we are having to wait!

Do you feel like you are waiting on God for something? Are you praying about a situation? Are you asking for something? Are you believing a certain circumstance will change? If so, you know what I mean.

Don't get me wrong. I am not hating on the waiting. In fact, I want to tell you how not to waste the waits and how to go through waiting seasons and come out better than you were when you went into them.

In the coffee shop that day, this guy and I began to talk about what we can do to keep from wasting the waiting season and not to feel like we are just hanging our heads and dragging our feet as we move through it. Since that conversation, I've even studied waiting seasons in the Bible, and I learned some great lessons I want to share from 2 Chronicles 7.

Since not many people are flipping to 2 Chronicles (although after this chapter, I hope you do!), I am going to summarize part of it. The main character in the story is Solomon, the son of King David. King David died at the end of 1 Chronicles, leaving Solomon to inherit the throne. You may remember Solomon. When he had a chance to ask God for anything, he asked only for wisdom. And he got it.

By the time we get to chapter 7, Solomon had become king of Israel. One of Solomon's purposes was to build a temple for the Lord. Even though we think of Solomon as this wise king, his dad, David, called Solomon young and inexperienced when he appointed him for this task (1 Chronicles 29:1). For the first six chapters of 2 Chronicles, we read about Solomon and the people's process of building. Let's just say this—just because you're waiting doesn't mean you won't be working! A lot of times what you're waiting for will be what you are working toward. Clear examples of this would be finishing school, working the entry-level position at your job, and reading books on healthy relationships while you wait on your future spouse.

After Solomon worked for seven years to complete the temple, we get to read the specifics of his prayer to God. Solomon knew that this temple he had built for the Lord really did not mean much if the Lord Himself did not show up. After seven years, he was waiting on the Lord's presence, praying for the Lord to hear his prayer.

One of the things that stuck out to me about Solomon's prayer is that even though he believed he was called to build this temple for the Lord, had clear direction from his dad that this was what he was supposed to do, and worked for seven years to complete it, he

> He is good.
> He is faithful.

still had doubts! In 2 Chronicles 6:18, Solomon said, "But will God really dwell on earth with humans? The heavens, even the highest heavens, cannot contain you. How much less this temple I have built!" After all of that, even Solomon questioned his purpose during the waiting season.

You can read the whole prayer in 2 Chronicles 6:14–42. In fact, I would encourage you to do that right now. When I read it, what also jumps out at me are all the times Solomon asked God to hear his prayer. In the New International Version of the Bible, he made that request twelve times. He prayed about what he wanted to happen in the temple, about what he didn't want, and about the kind of people he hoped Israel would be. So I feel confident in saying that he was serious about what he prayed, and he *really* wanted to know that God was listening.

Right after Solomon finished praying, God's presence filled the temple. Let's look at what happened next:

When all the people of Israel saw the fire coming down and the glorious presence of the LORD filling the Temple, they fell face down on the ground and worshiped and praised the LORD, saying,

"He is good!

His faithful love endures forever!"

Then the king and all the people offered sacrifices to the LORD. King Solomon offered a sacrifice of 22,000 cattle and 120,000 sheep and goats. And so the king and all the people dedicated the Temple of God. The priests took their assigned positions, and so did the Levites who were singing, "His faithful love endures forever!" They accompanied the singing with music from the instruments King David had made for praising the LORD. Across from the Levites, the priests blew the trumpets, while all Israel stood. . . .

For the next seven days Solomon and all Israel celebrated the Festival of Shelters. (2 Chronicles 7:3–6, 8 NLT).

The Spirit showed up! You might be thinking, *So why is this a message on waiting when Solomon did not have to wait very long?* God's Spirit showed up after Solomon's prayer, and that makes it seem like Solomon didn't wait long. But let me remind you of the *seven years* he worked. Solomon committed to building the temple. He worked hard on it. When he finished, he prayed passionately with his people for the temple, asking God repeatedly to hear him. He worked. He prayed. The Spirit showed up. He rejoiced. Then they had a full-on celebration—for seven days, as I would have too. They called it the Festival of Shelters, but I would call it a party. Everyone was eating, fellowshipping, worshipping, and dancing. The trumpets were blaring. All because they had completed their work and God's Spirit had entered the temple.

The people were super excited. And according to 2 Chronicles 7:10, after the celebration, "Solomon sent the people home. They were all joyful and glad because the Lord had been so good to David and to Solomon and to his people Israel" (NLT).

I want you to notice verse 12 in chapter 7 though. Remembering that Solomon had asked the Lord to hear him so many times, the response that we get to see is *huge*: "Then one night the Lord appeared to Solomon and said, '*I have heard your prayer* and have chosen this Temple as the place for making sacrifices'" (NLT).

Scripture doesn't tell us exactly when God appeared to Solomon, but it was at least eight days after he had prayed, probably more. God did not specifically answer Solomon's prayers immediately. He sent His Spirit and they rejoiced, but not until later did God respond. Yet what did they do while they waited for God to answer? They celebrated. They worshipped. They prayed. They presented their offerings. They came together as a community and praised God. And they declared His faithful love *before* He ever responded specifically with the words "I have heard your prayer."

I included this story in this chapter because I think we can learn a lot from how the Israelites responded to their own waiting season. They worked. They prayed. They rejoiced. Knowing they had a purpose to finish the temple was enough motivation for them to work hard in the long seven years of waiting. It kept them going. Knowing that God had been faithful before was enough for them to believe He would be faithful again. Knowing the Spirit of the Lord was with them was enough for them to rejoice in their waiting.

> Let's exchange the word *waiting* for *believing*.

Because the presence of the Lord was with them. They knew He was good. They knew He was faithful. They could say that before He even acknowledged having heard Solomon's prayer.

I am going to ask you some challenging questions about your season of waiting to see where you are and how you can shift your perspective.

What job are you in right now that seems like you will never be able to complete?

Where are you dragging your feet, wishing for another opportunity to come?

What are you waiting on that you are not praying for?

Is the Spirit of God being in you enough reason to rejoice even if God is not directly responding to you?

The apostle Paul had something to say about that in Philippians 4:4: "*Always* be full of joy in the Lord. I say it again—rejoice!" (NLT). Do you see that? He says we are to be joyful *always*, not just when we are happy.

The Message version of Philippians 4:4 makes this point even clearer: "Celebrate God all day, every day. I mean, *revel* in him!" All day, every day—not just on the days that go well for you but even when things are hard, even when you are worried, and even when you are waiting.

Notice that we are to revel in God. *Revel* means "noisy celebrations."[20] What do you think it would look like for people to have a noisy celebration of God's goodness all day, every day? I am speaking directly to Christians with this challenge: What do you think it says to people around us about the faithfulness of the God we believe in if we are always dragging our feet, drinking our lattes, complaining about the waiting? Let's exchange the word *waiting* for *believing*. Instead of being in a season of waiting, be in a season of believing. Today it would look like going about your everyday life with joy in your heart, with a smile on your face, and with peaceful confidence that God's goodness is about to be on display in your life in a major way.

In Solomon's day, celebrating noisily all day every day would probably look like a weeklong festival. Those people could celebrate because they understood that the presence of God was with them. Even though they had not directly experienced answers to their prayers, they still knew He was good. Even though He had not intervened yet, they knew He was working. Even though He had not specifically said, "I heard you when you prayed for this," they knew His presence was with them, and that was enough for them to worship. We can learn a lot from that.

You may look at my life and think God has answered me on every single prayer. You may think I do not have to wait on a thing, but that is not true. God has been so faithful to me and done things that have blown me away. I am forever grateful for these things, and I will praise Him for them, but there are several specific things that I am waiting for—or should I say believing for Him to answer—that I have not seen happen yet. However, because of how faithful I know He is, how good, and how fulfilled I am in His Spirit, my joy remains as I wait for the things to come.

DON'T LOSE YOUR BOLD,
COURAGEOUS FAITH, FOR YOU
ARE DESTINED FOR A GREAT
REWARD! YOU NEED THE
STRENGTH OF ENDURANCE TO
REVEAL THE POETRY OF GOD'S
WILL AND THEN YOU RECEIVE
THE PROMISE IN FULL. FOR
SOON AND VERY SOON, "THE
ONE WHO IS APPEARING WILL
COME WITHOUT DELAY!"

—HEBREWS 10:35-37 TPT

Don't Waste the Waiting: Part 2

I KNOW WE HAVE ALREADY TALKED A LOT ABOUT WHAT IT looks like to wait, but I want to share two practical ways to get through a waiting season without wasting it. I think it is important to talk about this because some sort of waiting will be a major part of our lives, and how we wait will determine how we are truly living. It will help us not just to remain alive but to *thrive*. Here are my two practical pieces of advice: first, focus on your relationship with God, and second, focus on what you already have.

1 Focus on your relationship with God.

We have a limited understanding of God, and sometimes we value our relationship with Him based only on what He's currently doing for us. This is sad but true, and it causes us to get twisted up about the timing of our celebrations. Let me explain what I mean.

Sometimes we say something like, "Okay, God. I am asking You for this. And depending on Your response, I will determine how I feel about our relationship."

We probably are not actually saying this verbally, but this is the way we are feeling deep down.

I don't think a healthy relationship with God works that way. The relationship comes first, and God's response—whether it's the one we want or not—gives us an opportunity to grow in our relationship with Him.

Waiting on an answer to prayer doesn't mean we have to just sit around. We can actively work on our relationship with God—just like when Solomon was building for seven years, he was praying and serving God during that time, actively seeking His presence. We can get to know God for just being God. We can get to know God's character and who He is. We can search His Word and seek out knowledge about Him. We can pray and seek His presence. We can seek the fruit of His Spirit in our everyday jobs. We can love those around us. We can discover that He is good and that His faithful love endures forever, no matter what. Then, based on knowing the character of who God is, we realize that by His grace we are worthy to go before His throne and ask Him for something. That's how it's supposed to work, but sometimes we flip it around. No shame in that. But in this waiting time, we have a chance to get it right.

Think about it this way. During the Christmas season, no seven-year-old says, "You know, I can hardly wait for Christmas because I'll get to spend quality time with my family. I can hardly wait to sit around the table enjoying a nice meal and then sing Christmas carols with the people I love."

No. The mind of a seven-year-old thinks, *I told Santa I want an Easy-Bake Oven, and if it's not under the tree, then I don't believe in him anymore.*

We can treat God the same way when we are not mature in our relationship with Him. We can easily think, *I told God I wanted that, and if He doesn't give it to me, then I am not going to believe in Him anymore—or at least I won't trust Him.*

This reminds me of the guy in the coffee shop who had told God what he wanted in terms of going to college

> By His grace we are worthy to go before His throne and ask Him for something.

and getting a job—and those things did not happen for him. He believed he deserved those things because he tried to obey God, but God doesn't give out presents based on a naughty and nice list. I told him this, and I will tell you the same thing: "This is going to be hard to hear, but the school you wanted and the job you want were never promises of God. There are a lot of promises from God you can hang on to, but the job and the school aren't included." Here is what *is* included. These are just a few promises His Word gives us:

He gives strength to the weary and increases the power of the weak. (Isaiah 40:29)

The Lord himself goes before you and will be with you; he will never leave you nor forsake you. (Deuteronomy 31:8)

The lions may grow weak and hungry, but those who seek the Lord lack no good thing. (Psalm 34:10)

"The thief comes only to steal and kill and destroy; I have come that they may have life, and have it to the full." (John 10:10)

When you've asked God for something and then find yourself waiting for Him to respond, don't let the seemingly slow response pull you away from Him. Realize that the timing of His answer is perfect, even if you can't see that right away. See that time as a gift that will allow you to grow deeper in your relationship with Him.

2 Focus on what you already have.

If you and I could look back through time and watch Israel celebrate during the Festival of Shelters, I think we would see everything that makes for a great party—lots of food, people enjoying each other, and dancing in the streets. We would hear the trumpets blasting praise to God and see people praising and worshipping everywhere. Was all of that because God had answered every one of their prayers the way they wanted Him to? Nope. But they celebrated because the presence of God was with them. They were completely focused on that, and it was worth a huge party.

You may want something from God right now, praying as hard as you know how to pray. Maybe, like the seven-year-old who wants an Easy-Bake Oven, that one thing is all you can think about. That's going to make the waiting difficult and unproductive. If you'll challenge yourself to think about other things, the time will seem to pass more quickly, and you will become stronger through this waiting season.

> Make a list of everything good in your life.

I have a suggestion for what you can think about. Think about all the good things you already have. Do you have a roof over your head and a bed to sleep in? Think about that. Do you have friends and family members who care about you? Think about them. Is there something you're good at and you enjoy doing? Think about

that. Do you know Jesus, and can you sense the presence of God? Think about that—*a lot*.

I challenge you to take your phone or a piece of paper and make a list of everything good in your life. Include all the seemingly little things. For example, do you have shoes on your feet? How good was that ice cream you ate last night before bed? When you think you've finished, ask yourself, "What else?" Do that a few times and make the list as long as you possibly can. As you think about these things and all the other blessings in your life, thank God for them. You may not think of these simple things as blessings, but I have been many places in the world where people do not have these things in their day-to-day life, yet they are grateful and still alive. Truly living is not a matter of what you have but rather the gratitude and contentment in your heart. When you write down this list and shift your perspective, your gratitude and contentment will grow. You'll find your heart wanting to praise Him instead of agonizing over the wait. You'll realize that all you really need in life is His presence and that He has given you that and so much more. Never forget what you do have as you wait for what you don't have yet.

Have Fun!

'M SERIOUS. YOU CAN HAVE FUN WHEN YOU'RE WAITING FOR something. I know the whole idea of waiting gets a bad rap, but it really can be fun. I've got an acronym for this: *Faith United Gets Noisy.* That's exactly what happened in ancient Israel.

You may be thinking, *Hmmm. Sadie must not know how to spell fun. She's got a* g *in it.* But I have a simple explanation. The *g* is silent. If we can get past the fact that the *g* in *gnat* is silent, then we should be able to get past a silent *g* in *fugn,* right? Feel free to ignore the *g* if you want. It's just there because it got me to *noisy.*

FAITH

Here's how to have fun in the waiting. First, have faith. If you have faith, a lot more things can be fun. In the same way, without faith life can get hard, confusing, and even miserable.

Let's start by asking, "What is faith?" It's defined in Hebrews 11:1, which is a life verse for me: "Now faith is confidence in what we hope for and assurance about what we do not see." The rest of Hebrews 11 then goes through a long list of people we know as heroes of faith—Abraham, Sarah, Joseph, Moses, Rahab, Gideon, and others.

You may have heard about these heroes of the Bible and their epic stories of faith. When we think about them, it's easy to say to ourselves, "I want to be a hero. I want that heroic kind of faith." Then we think that in order to be a hero, we need to do heroic things. So we start asking God to give us something amazing to do. We think if He will just do that, we can be the kind of hero we read about in the Bible. I always think about Moses when I think of biblical heroes. I love him! He was so scared of talking to Pharaoh that he actually tried to talk God out of sending him (I can relate), but when he finally stopped talking, listened to God, and did what He said, he brought his people out of slavery. He went up on a mountain and saw God. He split the Red Sea!

As I've studied these stories in the Bible, I've come to realize that the only thing separating you from the heroes of the Bible is faith. Being heroic is not about whether God answers a prayer the way you want or whether you do some amazing thing for Him. It's just about whether you believe in the One who can do the impossible.

If you have faith, trusting God with all your heart, that's what makes you a hero. If God gives you a great assignment or sends you somewhere or leads you to do something—whether it is speaking His Word to a stadium full of people, talking to a few people in a village in Africa, throwing a neighborhood garage sale and giving the money to the church mission, paying for the coffee of the person behind you, showing up for a friend who is hurting, sending a text to someone who needs it, or even posting an encouraging comment on someone's Instagram—and you obey that, that's what makes you a hero.

What I'm talking about here is kingdom-minded thinking and living. First of all, just knowing that you are part of something much bigger than yourself can give your life meaning. If you are a follower of God, then you are a part of His kingdom here on earth. You don't just have a purpose in heaven; His kingdom is right here and right now, and you have a role to play. Being kingdom-minded is not just thinking about your own plan—it is thinking about heaven's plan. Moses is a good example. Leading the people out of Egypt was definitely not Moses' plan, but God knew he was the one to get the job done. Kingdom-minded thinking does not look at the world the way we look at it, and it doesn't consider worldly values or status. No one else would have picked Moses for the job, because he was so afraid to speak, but God knew that Pharaoh would pay attention when he saw Moses. There is a total difference in a kingdom-minded perspective and a worldly perspective. To have a kingdom mind-set we have to have faith and surren-

> Being brave is about whether you believe in the One who can do the impossible.

der the idea of our own goal, our own dream, and our own heroic act and say, "God, I believe that whatever You say is not only good enough for me but is actually the perfect thing for my life and those around me. And it is going to bless more people than anything I could have thought of myself." Then, and only then, the most amazing things will happen.

The reason I relate myself to Moses is because I was so much like him. When I felt called to preach, I was so afraid. From my own perspective, I thought I might go into acting. It made sense. It was fun, and there was an opportunity there, but I felt God shift me into something else, and that was scary. Now that I have been able to see the kingdom impact my yes to God's call has made, I am so thankful that I chose to trust His direction. Your yes matters, especially

when that yes is fueled by faith that God has the power to do in and through you what He has called you to. It will help us make the most of the life we have.

Luke 1:37 (NKJV) tells us there is nothing that is impossible for God. That sentence contains two key words: *for God.* Many things are impossible for us, but nothing is impossible for Him. In order to get the benefits of that verse, we have to partner with God and have faith. It matters.

Someone once told me something that changed my life and the way I pray: "Sadie, you just need to ask God to give you the faith to believe." I heard those words at a time when I was toeing the line between saying yes to what God had called me to and staying comfortable. Those simple words struck me, convicted me, and made me think, *Ask God for faith?* Before I heard that encouragement, I had felt that the one thing I could do for God was to have faith. I knew that He could give me peace and joy and other things. In fact, He has given me everything.

> Ask God to give you the faith to believe.

He has sent His Son for me. Couldn't I at least give Him faith? I thought my job, so to speak, as a Christian was that I was just supposed to have a lot of faith and a lot of hope and to believe and not doubt.

But then I realized that in the New Testament, even the apostles asked God to increase their faith. God actually wants to help us with that. Sometimes I think He would like for us to know that He wants to do so much for us. That He understands it is hard to believe. That what He wants to do for us is so much bigger than anything we could even hope for, think of, or imagine (Ephesians 3:20). That's why He wants to give us the faith to believe.

If you're struggling with faith, I want to encourage you to ask God to give you the faith to believe. You can also pray that He will give you the strength that you need or that He'll help you believe that you are loved and that you are enough. Or maybe it goes deeper, and you need to ask Him for the faith to believe that your life matters and your breath has purpose. That's not too far-out to ask God for. That's not crazy. It's exactly what God wants you to do.

I did experience a shift when I began to ask God for faith. I felt peace when I preached. I felt carried when I danced. I had confidence when I walked into seasons of waiting. I did not stress as much when things got overwhelming. Our God delivers for us, friends!

UNITED

In John 17, one of Jesus' last prayers during His earthly ministry, He prayed for unity. We have to believe that if Jesus prayed something, it mattered. He prayed that you and I would be united with the Father. What does this mean? Let's read from John 17:11, 20–21 (TPT):

> "Holy Father, I am about to leave this world to return and be with you, but my disciples will remain here. So I ask that by the power of your name, protect each one that you have given me, and watch over them so that they will be united as one, even as we are one. . . . And I ask not only for these disciples, but also for all those who will one day believe in me through their message. I pray for them all to be joined together as one even as you and I, Father, are joined together as one. I pray for them to become one with us so that the world will recognize that you sent me."

The very nature of God is unity. He is three in one: Father, Son, and Spirit. Since the very beginning of creation, God formed human life so that we could be in a relationship with Him. Once sin entered the world, we became distant from God because sin separates us. The reason God sent His Son, Jesus, to die on the cross was to redeem the very essence of why we exist—to be in a relationship with Him. We are saved by Jesus' sacrifice, and we enter the family of God and receive the gift of the Spirit. God loves you so much that He would go to any lengths, even to the extent of seeing His Son on the cross, to bring you back into unity with Him. Through this we are all united under the same blood that saved us all by grace. That's the Bible in a nutshell, and that's why Jesus prayed that His disciples would be one. When we are united with the Father and live as one on the earth, then we are fulfilling what we were created to do.

In Matthew 18:20, Jesus says, "Where two or three gather in my name, there am I with them." Do you believe that? Do you believe that every time you gather with other Christians, He is there? He is. That's an awesome thought. I can remember so many times on my Live Original tour when everyone worshipped together, and I felt a sense of what heaven is going to feel like. There have even been times when I've prayed with some friends and felt total peace in His presence as we called out to Him.

I can't encourage you strongly enough to seek unity. Gather with people. Believe with people. Pray with them. Ask your friends, "What are you waiting on? Let's pray into it. Let's believe for it." Don't be afraid. Don't think, *What if it doesn't happen?* That's where faith comes in. Have faith; have hope. A part of faith is believing that God is good, even when we don't get that Easy-Bake Oven. Be part of believing together for God to do something great in someone's life and in this world.

Believe with people.

I can almost hear what you may be thinking: *Okay, but what if I get together with someone and I pray and believe—and then nothing happens? What if God doesn't come through? Then does He look bad?* I get it. Praying and believing can seem risky sometimes. But here's what I have learned about that: you and I do not have to try to save God's reputation. We aren't responsible for results. We're only responsible for asking in faith. Besides, praying with faith and a pure heart can never make God look bad. He is holy, holy, holy. The angels say that in heaven day and night. He has always been—and will always be—beautiful and powerful and strong.

So go ahead and be bold. Find someone and get together and pray. Stir up your faith to believe for what you do not see. And watch God work.

NOISY

In Solomon's day, the people were noisy. Just think about the sounds around the temple during those seven days when the Israelites partied. The trumpets were blaring, people were singing, and I'm sure people were talking and laughing, and children were playing too. They were giving God glory in a loud way. That's such a powerful example for you and me. We *have* to worship God with passion. We *have* to pray with intensity and to be bold in what we ask of God. Why? Because in God's presence, there is enough to praise. Even if He hasn't yet done what we've prayed He will do, there's already enough to praise Him for—and to make some noise about it—just because He is with us.

When I think about getting noisy, one word that comes to mind is *enthusiastic*. I mean, you don't often think about enthusiastic people being still and quiet, right? There's usually a good bit of activity that goes with having enthusiasm.

Sometimes the temptation in the waiting season is to drag our feet and be passive. We just want to walk around thinking, *Oh, what's the Lord doing? I'm in a season of waiting. I think I'll have a latte.* But Romans 12:11–12 says, "Never be lazy, but work hard and serve the Lord enthusiastically. Rejoice in our confident hope. Be patient in trouble, and keep on praying" (NLT).

Fight the temptation to be lazy. Work hard. Serve the Lord. Keep on praying. And do it all with enthusiasm.

No one gets exactly what they want exactly when they want it. Everyone has to wait for something, and part of what distinguishes us as Christians from people who do not know the Lord is the way we wait. What message do we send to them when they see us waiting but not doing it very well? Anyone can *not* do it well, but we are called to do it with excellence and enthusiasm. People who don't know Jesus have to wait and wonder what will happen. They have a reason to be nervous! But we don't.

And really, we have a whole lot already. We can worship. There are people to talk to and things to pray for. And it doesn't have to be in some exotic place. It doesn't have to be on a platform. It can literally be in your school cafeteria. It can be on the phone with a friend, saying, "Hey, I've just been thinking about you. I'm praying for you. What are you believing for? What are you going through?"

Living with enthusiasm can be as simple as having a conversation. Let's be excited. We have *so much* to be loud about.

One of the Bible verses I love is Psalm 30:11, which says that God has turned our "mourning into joyful dancing" (NLT). This is something the Spirit of God does for us, and we can believe Him for that. But we often think, *Okay, I know God turns mourning into dancing, but when is it going to happen?*

We can be tempted to believe that maybe God will turn our mourning into dancing after He responds to what we're asking for. I don't think that's necessarily true. I think God will turn our mourning into dancing when we simply rest in His presence, when we rest in the joy of who He is.

Joy is a fruit of the Holy Spirit (Galatians 5:22–23). It's something God provides for your life, and it can be with you every single day. That doesn't mean there won't be times when you are sad or when you feel things. Some situations are going to hurt; things are going to happen; friendships are going to change. Being joyful does not mean avoiding the circumstances that can bring pain or sadness. It means that during those hard times there will be a deep inner joy that will continue through them. The Bible doesn't say that when everything in your life is amazing, you can have joy. It says, as the psalmist sings to God, "Your presence is fullness of joy" (Psalm 16:11 NKJV).

You won't always know when your answer from God is coming, and that is hard sometimes because you're *really* believing and you're *really* hoping. Even though you can't schedule it and you don't know when to expect it, you can still live in freedom. You can live with joy.

I think about the girls in juvie—the place where we threw the dance party. They are *literally* in a waiting season in a confined place.

> God will turn our mourning into dancing.

But because we had a dance party, I watched freedom rise up in a room of girls who are in a season of waiting to be released. One type of freedom is coming to them someday, but another type they can experience right where they are, right now. On the day we danced, I watched the most awkward, dead room suddenly spring to life with joy and freedom.

Their lives and mine could not be more different. But that did not drive us apart, because we all aligned with one truth—that the same God is our Father. And that there is freedom, joy, peace, friendship, and relationship anywhere the presence of God is. No matter how different people may be or what scenarios you may find yourself in, you can worship, you can dance, and you can be free—just because His presence enters the room.

No matter what your waiting season looks like, no matter how dead your dreams may feel right now, and no matter how awkward it may feel to start dancing, worshipping, and praising God, I encourage you to do it. Before He even directly answers your prayers, keep dancing, keep worshipping, and keep praising. Because when you feel His presence, it will change everything. It's going to give you a reason to have faith and believe again, to celebrate and unite with other people. For some, it will provide a reason to just keep going. Wherever you are, whatever you're going through, find God's presence in it. Because that is all you really need. In John 15:7, Jesus says, "If you remain in me and my words remain in you, ask whatever you wish, and it will be done for you."

> Keep dancing,
> keep worshipping,
> and keep praising.

I want God to answer everything that's in your heart. But I also know that God is so good and so faithful that if His presence is with you, then you have *everything*. His provision in your life will be exactly what you need. You won't go without anything.

I'm not talking about some kind of spiritual high but about a spiritual awakening that draws you into deeper trust and deeper satisfaction in all He offers you, no matter what your circumstances may be.

Celebrate

ONE OF MY FAVORITE WORDS IS *CELEBRATE*. NOT LONG AGO, at the beginning of the year, some friends and I decided to choose a word to focus on for the next twelve months. I chose *celebration*. When I first started telling people about that, some of them roasted me for it. Everyone else was choosing words like *surrender, sacrifice, build, faith*—you know, really serious words. They didn't think my word was very spiritual. Plus, I celebrate all the time. I do. I love to throw a party for no reason. I just think almost everything is worth celebrating. I love laughter and good times. When we know God, we have more reasons to celebrate than we can count.

One definition of *celebrate* is to "honor or praise publicly," and I've been thinking about this a lot as I read the Bible.[21] The book of Revelation paints the most amazing picture of God's throne in heaven. Surrounding His throne are twenty-four elders, and in the center are four living creatures who never stop worshipping Him. Day and night, they say, "'Holy, holy, holy is the Lord God Almighty,' who was, and is, and is to come" (Revelation 4:8).

My takeaway from this is that no matter what I step into or what my day looks like, I can be joyful. Because I know my God is holy, I can publicly honor and praise Him as I celebrate each day. I've recently learned a lot about celebration that I didn't understand before. I will celebrate when there's something to celebrate. I am going to celebrate when my friends are together and when everything is going well. But I'm learning to celebrate when things are not great. This can be much more difficult, but if we think about celebration as honoring or praising our Father in heaven, then it's something we can do no matter what our current circumstance is.

> If you can look at the big picture, you can find a way to celebrate.

There were times within the year that I would think to myself, *Shoot, why did I pick this word?* There were days it was hard to feel the desire to celebrate, but I had to figure out how to shift my mindset. Here is a small example: I travel a lot, and there was a trip that I took in the year of "celebration" that was not only a multicity trip; I also went to another country. I went to Israel, Ohio, and Colorado. Israel and Ohio were work trips that involved filming a Bible study series and preaching in front of a lot of teens.

My bag never showed up. When I say it did not show up, I mean not in Israel, not in Ohio, not in Colorado. I spent the two weeks borrowing everything I needed from literal strangers, and when I say everything, I mean *everything*. During this time I was trying to be grateful for where I was and positive about the things I had, trying to shift my mind to remember my word—*celebration*—but when I finally got my bag back when I got home, my brand-new suitcase had a gash in the middle of it, and my hair products had burst and

stained my new clothes. Let's just say I did not want to jump up and down in excitement. I looked at my new things that had been ruined, and I was challenged by what my response was going to be. I ended up bleaching my clothes and laughing about it, and to this day, I get complimented on those bleached clothes.

It is easy to let the little things that don't go the way you planned steal your celebration. If you can look past your annoyance in the moment and look at the big picture, you can find a way to celebrate. You may even find that those little changes you were not expecting introduced you to new people or made things better. Keep your perspective up—it's not being naïve; it's just being happy. I hope that becomes a reason you can celebrate too.

> Celebrate God all day, every
> day. I mean *revel* in him!
> —Philippians 4:4 MSG

Happy Birthday!

ONE TIME I PLANNED A BIRTHDAY PARTY FOR A VERY GOOD friend, someone I love dearly. As her birthday drew near, she made it clear that she was not excited about this one. The closer it got, the sadder she became, until she eventually told me to call off the party. When I asked her why, she said, "I just don't feel like my life is worth celebrating." I was crushed that she felt that way, but I went ahead and canceled the party to honor what she wanted.

Just to keep things real with you, I need to tell you that I was angry about all of this—not angry with her but angry at the lie the Enemy had convinced her to believe. Kind of like the anger I had when Christian said he sucks. My friend is an incredible person, and the Enemy had blinded her to that on her birthday. She is so special to so many people, but she ended up in a funk, feeling alone and unlovable—then making things worse by not allowing her friends to be with her and show her how much we love her. (Sometimes we dig our own pit.) She is the kind of friend who is the life of everyone else's party, but when it came to her own party, she did not even feel she was worth celebrating.

On the day of her birthday, I had no idea what to do. On the one hand, I wanted to honor her request to ignore the day. On the other hand, I wanted her to know she is loved and worth at least a gift. I prayed about it and asked God what to get her. (By the way, nothing is too silly or simple to pray for. He is *so* into the details.) Then I got an idea.

I gave her two cards.

She opened the first one, which said on the outside, "This is a card about nothing." On the inside, I simply wrote, "Love ya! Sadie" and added the date. It was almost as bad as someone replying "K" to a text message. When she opened it, I said, "This is to honor the day you wanted to have." She read it and laughed sarcastically.

When I gave her the second card, which was more like a mini-journal, I said, "This one is to honor you as a friend." On the front it said, "What if . . ." On the first blank page I wrote, "What if you saw yourself the way everyone around you sees you? Then I can promise you that you would know how worth a celebration you are."

That day happened to be her thirty-first birthday, so in the card I wrote a list of thirty-one reasons I wanted to celebrate her. She read it and wept. She later told me that on the night of her birthday, she read over all thirty-one of the reasons she is worth celebrating and said that was the first night she had ever realized and believed she is lovable. Remember, words do hold the power of *life*.

I have other friends who have also struggled with their birthdays. One didn't want to celebrate her most recent milestone because she had just broken up with a guy. For her, I went to where she was and started a dance party. I also gave her some hilarious gifts

pertaining to her future boyfriend. To this day, she says that birthday has been her favorite one.

Another friend didn't want to acknowledge her birthday because she had just walked through some very difficult situations. I found out what her favorite meal is and made sure it was on her table that night with a card about all the wonderful things her life means to me.

The gift of life
was the first gift
you ever received.

I get it. Things happen. And some of those things are really hard and painful. They can make us feel like the last thing we ever want to do is celebrate, especially if we let whether things are going well for us determine our level of celebration. The minute we compare our celebration-worthiness to others or even to our personal estimation of significance, it strips us of our ability to celebrate life to the fullest. Again, this reminds me of when the older brother in the story of the prodigal son compared his life to his brother's. For you it may be the boy or the gifts you didn't get or the nagging feeling that your life is just not worth being celebrated.

No matter what you have been through or what you have believed about yourself, I want to say that birthdays are special.

Let me get personal and make a couple of points about *your* birthday.

For starters, the gift of life was the first gift you ever received. Most likely, you were celebrated just because you came into the world, before you ever did anything worth celebrating. Even if people on earth did not celebrate you, I *know* heaven was celebrating. Remember, God created us because He wanted a relationship with us. Go read Psalm 139 if you are doubting that. God knew you before you were formed in your mother's womb, He saw you, He has always had a plan for you, and your life was written in His book before you took your first breath. Verses 17 and 18 of that psalm read, "How precious are your thoughts about me, O God. They cannot be numbered! I can't even count them; they outnumber the grains of sand!" (NLT).

Your birthday is a reminder that God gave you life. It gives you a fresh start every year. It symbolizes the fact that there was something about God's image that He wanted to create in you and share with the world. If you are like my friend and you do not yet believe you are worthy of celebration, I want to remind you that your birthday is the ultimate affirmation of who you are and why your life matters.

We can often tell if something we believe about ourselves is a lie by looking back to the days when we were little and asking if the younger version of ourselves would have believed it. Almost every child's favorite day of the year is his or her birthday. It means a party, cake, attention, and gifts! But somewhere along the way, we can allow the Enemy's language of lies to take away the beauty and celebration of who we are.

I hope this has helped you. When your birthday rolls around, it's time to party!

Boom! Roasted

THERE'S ONE THING YOU CAN BE SURE OF: YOU WILL NOT DO everything right. At some point, you'll have an epic fail, or you'll at least make a mistake or do something others think is funny or stupid or weird. People will notice, and some of them won't let you forget it. It may even be on social media, where the whole world could have access to it.

If you do anything that involves other people in any capacity, you "risk" being roasted. I put quotation marks around "risk" because it's not just a possibility. It's more of a fact. There *will* be times all of us will be picked on or made fun of. I say that not to be a downer, but to say this: don't let the fear of being roasted stop you from doing something you are excited about doing!

People roast people. It happens to me all the time. There are YouTube videos out there with hundreds of thousands of views of me being roasted and verbally picked apart. There are hundreds of comments saying that I sound annoying when I talk. Do those things hurt me? Sure. Because I'm human, and sometimes the comments sting. But I don't let those little stings stop me from doing what I love to do and from using my voice in the spaces where God opens doors for me to speak.

You don't have to let the fear of being roasted stop you either. You don't want to be silenced because a group of people who are choosing to focus on your mistakes or point out qualities that aren't your best when you could be saying something that could change someone's life and affect eternity. You don't want the haters to hold you back from fulfilling your calling.

So, if you have a desire in your heart to do something, but you're afraid you'll be roasted, I say: Do it anyway! If negative comments come, then they come. But don't let that stop you from doing what makes you, you! And certainly don't let it quiet your voice!

Boom! Go for it!

Don't let negative comments stop you from doing what makes you, you!

Comebacks
to the Haters

WHEN YOU START REALLY LIVING, YOU WILL HAVE HATERS. Would you believe there was a time when no one ever thought much about the word *haters*? Seriously. My grandparents and even my parents did not grow up using that word. But now when we hear it, we know exactly what it means. If I just said that one word, *hater*, to you, you would probably see someone's face immediately in your mind's eye or hear in your head a comment a hater has thrown at you.

Even though the terminology is relatively new, the concept of haters is not. They have been around since Old Testament times, as far back as Genesis. Cain was such a hater of his brother Abel that he killed him. Joseph's brothers hated on him and sold him as a slave. At least our haters just comment on our Instagram posts. I could list many other examples, but the story I want to focus on right now is about Nehemiah. Yes, even in the book of Nehemiah we have a hater-spotting. You can almost guarantee that anytime a person becomes a leader, as Nehemiah did, haters will come into the narrative.

In the story, Nehemiah wept, mourned, and fasted because the Jewish people were suffering, the walls of the city of Jerusalem were broken down, and the city gates were burned (Nehemiah 1:3). After a fervent time of prayer, Nehemiah realized he needed to go to Jerusalem to oversee the rebuilding of the wall; however, at the time, he worked as the cupbearer to the king. A cupbearer's job entailed standing beside the king and serving him drinks. This may not sound like that prestigious of a job, but you had to have a noble character if you were a cupbearer because you made sure the king's drinks were not poisoned. If the king had any fear that his drink had been poisoned, you would be called on to drink it first. If you didn't die, then the king knew it was safe for him to drink. I don't think this is a job I would sign up for, but it was a coveted position in the kingdom.

> As you step into your purpose, you will run into haters too.

As Nehemiah faithfully served in his position, he prayed that God would give him favor with the king so the king would allow him to take a leave of absence from the palace to get the wall built (v. 11). The king granted his request.

You might think that since Nehemiah viewed his work on the wall as something God had paved the way for, it would come easily to him. Well, not exactly. Nehemiah was a cupbearer, but he was a cupbearer with a willing heart, one who did not limit what God could and would do through him. In fact, as Nehemiah embraced his purpose to build the wall, he also ran into major haters named Sanballat and Tobiah.

Let me stop here and say that the same principle will probably apply to you. The Enemy's tactics have not changed. As you step into your purpose, you will run into haters too.

These haters of Nehemiah's day were no different than the ones you and I encounter in our day. But Nehemiah handled the hate by knowing what he was up against ("Hater Strategy 101") and not giving in to their tactics ("Comeback Strategy 101").

Nehemiah hadn't even met Sanballat and Tobiah when they first decided they didn't like him. Nehemiah 2:10 says, "They were very much disturbed that someone had come to promote the welfare of the Israelites."

Hate often starts as soon as you get the confidence to try to do something you are called to do. If the Enemy can stop you before you start, it would be the ultimate win for him.

HATER STRATEGY #1:

Haters will try to make you question what you are doing.

When the hate first comes against you, it may be in the form of little comments and questions. It may even seem like he or she is trying to help you out. Tobiah and Sanballat started by questioning Nehemiah. "'What is this you are doing?' they asked. 'Are you rebelling against the king?'" (Nehemiah 2:19). See that? They didn't threaten Nehemiah right off the bat; they brought the king into it, as though the king would be upset with him. They acted as if they didn't want him to get into trouble with the king. This tactic is as old as time. Satan used it in the garden of Eden when he said to Eve, "Did God really say, 'You must not eat from any tree in the garden'?" (Genesis 3:1). With that simple question he placed the doubt in Eve's mind that led to the fall of man.

COMEBACK STRATEGY #1:

Be confident in what you are doing.

Nehemiah didn't fall for it. He stood firm and put them in their place, saying, "The God of heaven will give us success. We his servants will start rebuilding, but as for you, you have no share in Jerusalem or any claim or historic right to it" (Nehemiah 2:20).

Nehemiah let them know that he had God on his side. Romans 8:31 says, "If God is for us, who can be against us?" Our confidence doesn't come from ourselves but from God who is with us. I am inspired by the quiet confidence these heroes in the Bible had. Even though he had to endure all that nagging and hating, Nehemiah did not get worked up—he just stated the facts. If God is for you, no hater can stop you. So do not let them get you all worked up.

> Stay confident. Never forget where your confidence comes from.

I've got to say, I may not have responded that calmly. It is a good thing that I was not the person in these Bible stories, because Exodus 14 would have said, "Bye, haters! You better watch this sea split!" Joshua 6 would have read, "Hey, hater, enjoy these seven days because this wall is coming down!" And the Lord knows, if I were Nehemiah, I would have been singing, "The praises are going up, and so is this wall, baby!"

One of my favorite life verses is Hebrews 10:35–36: "Do not throw away this confident trust in the Lord. Remember the great reward it brings you! Patient endurance is what you need now, so that you will continue to do God's will. Then you will receive all that he has promised" (NLT).

Stay confident, but never forget exactly where that confidence is coming from.

HATER STRATEGY #2:

Haters will belittle.

Nehemiah and the Jews continued to build the wall, but the comments didn't stop. Sanballat called them "feeble Jews," and Tobiah said, "What they are building—even a fox climbing up on it would break down their wall of stones!" (Nehemiah 4:2–3).

When haters comment, they do it to belittle us, discourage us, shame us, or cause us to be afraid. Sanballat and Tobiah's comments are so ridiculous that it's obvious to us what they are trying to do. It's literally laughable how ludicrous they are. Isn't it strange how when someone says something hateful to someone else, we can see it for what it is so clearly? But when someone does it to us, even things that sound as dumb as "a fox could break it" can sometimes hurt.

I remember in the very early days of *Duck Dynasty*, I read a comment where someone said I looked like a man. I was a fifteen-year-old girl at the time, so this comment was absurd, but somehow it stung. I told Mom that night about it, and she replied, "Well, I read a comment today where someone said I look like Squidward from *SpongeBob*, so at least you aren't a six-armed squid. I think I win." We both died laughing at how silly the haters can be, and I resolved not to let the ridiculous comments online stop us from what we were doing.

COMEBACK STRATEGY #2:

Keep working with all your heart.

At this point in the story, Nehemiah and his people had built the wall to half of its intended height. Nehemiah 4:6 says they "worked with all their heart."

When hate comes against you, just stay focused and keep working as hard as you can. Colossians 3:23–24 says, "Whatever you do, work at it with all your heart, as working for the Lord, not for human masters, since you know that you will receive an inheritance from the Lord as a reward. It is the Lord Christ you are serving."

You aren't doing what you're doing for the haters anyway. Your work is not for them. It's for the Lord, so keep going!

HATER STRATEGY #3:

Haters try to take out leaders.

When we rise to a God-given opportunity, we need to be aware that opposition may arise against us. Nehemiah was the one with the burden and the grace to rebuild the walls. Many Jews worked on various portions of the wall, but all of them looked to Nehemiah

for direction and inspiration. Sanballat and Tobiah knew that if they could take out Nehemiah, they could stop the Israelites' progress. Whether you are in an official leadership position or not, you are the leader of whatever God has called you to do. In that position, you're vulnerable to hate.

The more Sanballat and Tobiah tried—and failed—to stop the work on the wall, the more creative they got. After the wall was completed but before the gates had been restored, they sent Nehemiah a message: "Come, let us meet together in one of the villages on the plain of Ono" (Nehemiah 6:2). The first time I read Nehemiah 6, I laughed out loud. The plain of Ono? Some of the place names in the Bible are hard to pronounce, but this one is simple. You can sound it out yourself: *oh no!* Something tells me he shouldn't go!

COMEBACK STRATEGY #3:

Decline their invitation.

Nehemiah knew they were up to no good, and he would not stand for it. He sent them a message saying, "I am carrying on a great project and cannot go down. Why should the work stop while I leave It and go down to you?" (Nehemiah 6:3).

Let me just say to you that you do not have to accept the invitation of the Enemy. Distractions have a sound, a certain ring, to them. When they come, we recognize them, just like Nehemiah did, and I want to encourage you to know the sound of your distraction. For some people, it's certain websites. For some, it's a group of people. For some, it's social media. For some, it's a person outside of your relationship. If you know that something will lead you into danger or temptation, it's time to say, "Oh no," and do not go!

> Your work is for the Lord, so keep going!

When you are walking with God, your whole life is a great project, so stay focused on that. I love how Nehemiah responds to the haters. "I'm doing a great work, so why would I stop this and go with you?" You can respond the same way when you get the offer to go to the plain of Ono in your life. Simply remind yourself that God is doing a great work in you. Why would you stop that to go hang out with the haters? Oh no, don't go! You can decline the invitation from the Enemy.

HATER STRATEGY #4:

Haters are persistent.

Sanballat and Tobiah were definitely persistent! They did not take "oh no" for an answer. In fact, they sent Nehemiah the same invitation four times, and four times he gave them the same response (Nehemiah 6:4).

Your haters may be persistent too. They will try to outlast you. If so, remember Nehemiah's strategy and continue to say no to the haters no matter how many times they try.

COMEBACK STRATEGY #4:

Pray.

Nehemiah knew where God was moving, and he was committed to staying right in the middle of it. If you read the entire book of Nehemiah, you'll see that his main leadership strategy was prayer. From start to finish, he sought God. God gave him everything he needed to keep the others motivated, to stand against the haters, and to finish the work He laid on his heart.

When the haters come into your life, lay them at God's feet. He is big enough to handle them.

HATERS STRATEGY #5:

Haters try to overcome their own insecurity by bringing you down.

Okay, maybe this isn't so much a strategy of the haters as it is a truth about them. It was certainly a characteristic of Nehemiah's enemies, and I can bet it's a truth about yours. Was there ever a time when *you* were the hater? Can you think about what was behind that? Many times we try to bring others down when we are feeling bad about ourselves. Recognize that in yourself and stop it before it starts. Don't allow your own insecurities to lead you to be the hater.

COMEBACK STRATEGY #5:

Guard yourself against the hater's schemes.

In Nehemiah 4:14, Nehemiah tells the people, "Don't be afraid of them. Remember the Lord, who is great and awesome, and fight for your families, your sons and your daughters, your wives and your homes." Nehemiah stationed people all around the wall to protect themselves from the enemies. They worked together to develop a strategy for protection. You can do this too. First, trust in God, who is great and awesome; second, surround yourself with people who will fight for you. The Israelites had a system where they would call out with a loud trumpet if they saw an enemy approaching. Make sure there are friends in your life who will do this for you. If you don't have those friends, ask God to place them in your life and then begin to be that friend to someone else.

Finally, the Israelites completed the wall. Nehemiah 6:15–16 says, "So the wall was completed. . . . When all our enemies heard about this, all the surrounding nations were afraid and lost their self-confidence, because they realized that this work had been done with the help of our God." I love that it says that the enemies "were afraid and lost their self-confidence."

Genesis 50:20 says, "You intended to harm me, but God intended it for good to accomplish what is now being done." The haters may mean to harm you, but if you stick with God, He promises to turn it into something good.

There are so many stories of haters in the Bible. You might not find that term in there, but I can assure you they are there. As you are reading, you'll be able to spot them and see how the people in these great stories handled them. Jesus faced the most haters of any of us. They said all kinds of bad things about Him and questioned Him relentlessly to try to stop Him from teaching the truth, and, ultimately, He was hated to the point that they crucified Him.

> Don't let the haters stop you from fully living.

Since He is the perfect Son of God and He got hate, how could we expect to be immune from it ourselves?

Know that as you go through life, encountering haters is unavoidable, but if you have these comeback strategies ready, you will not let them stop you from fully living and doing the things God calls you to do.

No Comparison

IN 1 THESSALONIANS 5:11, PAUL WROTE TO THE BELIEVERS, "Encourage one another and build each other up, just as in fact you are doing." Do you see what he is saying? Keep building each other up, *"just as in fact you are doing."* These words convict me. Paul wrote them so boldly, as if the Thessalonian Christians were already doing it. He didn't tell them to *begin* building each other up; he told them to *keep* doing it.

I wonder: If Paul wrote a letter to the church today, would he phrase it that way? Could he say that we are already building each other up? Or would he say, "You all really should start building each other up and encouraging each other. You are not each other's enemy. You have an Enemy. Don't take each other out. Keep each other going strong."

This is such an important message for our generation of Christians. We need each other. We need to start building up each other and keep doing it.

As I thought about this verse after reading it one day, I asked myself what would keep us from building up one another. What is it that causes us to tear each other down?

There may be more than one answer to those questions, but I know this: if we want to build each other up, comparison has to go. If we compare ourselves with others, we are looking at each other and sizing each other up, saying, "Who's better at this? Who's not good at this?" When this happens, we are not looking at each other with the lens of Jesus.

Instead, we need to have confidence in who we are and in what God's doing in our lives so we can cheer on our sisters and brothers. If she is doing an amazing thing and he is doing an amazing thing, it doesn't make what I am doing any less amazing. It makes us all winning for the kingdom of God.

Let me encourage you to restructure your mind to think that you, your sister, and your brother are all running the same race. That's a kingdom mind-set, which is the path to truly living. When Jesus taught us how to pray, He said these words: "Your kingdom come, your will be done, on earth as it is in heaven" (Matthew 6:10). A kingdom mind-set is one that strives for God's will to be done right here, right now, on earth. It's not about waiting until we're all in heaven and made perfect and the pain has gone away. It is the mind-set that we have a job to do right here to advance God's kingdom on earth as it is in heaven. If you can have a kingdom mind-set, you won't be so disappointed when your worldly status doesn't seem as impressive as that of the person beside you. In fact, you won't even think about comparing yourself to other people because you will be so busy cheering them on.

> We have a job to do right here to advance God's kingdom on earth.

The first book I wrote is called *Live Original*. The word *original* means much more to me now than it did when I wrote that book, and it has become a part of almost everything I do—my website, our tour, everything I speak about. With so many people all searching for identity, we need to be reminded that we are all created in the image of God (Genesis 1:27). We are His original masterpieces. I really want you to understand what the word *original* means and how it applies to comparison.

O·RIG·I·NAL / ∃'RIJƎNL / *adjective*

1. Present or existing from the beginning; first or earliest.

2. Created personally by a particular artist; not a copy.[22]

Do you see the end of the second definition? It says, "Not a copy." So let me ask you this: What is it that drives us to compare ourselves with others? Yep, it's usually the desire to copy or imitate someone— someone we think is prettier, smarter, more athletic, more popular, or more together. If each of us existed on our own little planet, with no one else to look at, there would be no comparison. We'd also be very lonely, but that's not what I want to address here. My point is that we are created to live in community with other people. They are intended to bless us, as we are meant to bless them, but we can end up cursing each other because we are busy comparing instead of celebrating the good in one another. That's not God's plan.

So what is God's plan? We can begin to see it when we think about Him as the Creator and about ourselves as His creations. He is the original Creator. There was not one before Him. He's existed from before the beginning, and He is not a copy or an imitation.

God was the first to create. He made all of creation and designed and crafted each of us with amazing individuality. God saw no need to compare one of us with another one. He was only focused on making us unique. If you don't believe me, just put this book down for a minute and look around you. Do you look exactly like anything or anyone you see? Even if you're an identical twin, there are still differences!

In addition, we know that everything God made is good (1 Timothy 4:4). So you and I, God's creations, are good, and we are made just as He wanted and chose to make us. This leaves no room for the complete lie of comparison. Comparison was not a part of God's creative process, so it should not be a part of what was created. It's an offense to what God created and calls "good."

If we read Genesis 1 carefully, we notice that after God made every single part of creation, the Bible says, "It was good." But the man, Adam, was not good all by himself. Only when God created a woman, Eve, did the two of them become good together. The man needed someone who was different than he was in order to enter into goodness.

God's intention in creating Eve was not for Adam to compare himself to her or to compete with her. His divine design was for the two of them to come together for something good. This teaches us that comparison has no place in the life or thinking of anyone God has made. Everything God created was good—one thing wasn't better than anything else.

> We are created to live in community with other people.

The same adjective, *good*, is used for all of it. He didn't say the sun was "amazing" and the moon was "awesome." It was all "good."

What's interesting to me about the creation story is that it includes the sun, the moon, the waters, the animals, *and* humanity. We're all part of the same narrative, crafted by the same Creator. Yet

| **We need**
| **one another.**

you and I are not tempted to compare ourselves with the sun or the moon or the oceans. Seriously. If you were to hear someone say, "I feel less-than because the sun shines brighter than I ever will" or "I'm just not as deep as the ocean, and I can't get over it" or "I'm jealous of oxen because they are stronger than I am," you would think that was crazy! No one says things like that. We understand that we are all part of the same creation. Although human beings are the highest creations (Psalm 8:3–6), we realize that we need everything else God made. The sun and the oceans keep us alive. They enable us to reside and remain on earth. We need them. And we certainly need one another.

God created each of us, and none of us is better than anyone else. We're all good. Next time you're tempted to compare, remember that while you may think someone else is better than you are, that's just a lie. That person is good, and you are just as good.

When I think about how much some people compare themselves to others and struggle to view themselves as good—wanting a different nose, a different voice, or a different waistline—it breaks my heart. They are missing out on something so beautiful and so special—themselves!

Genesis 1:27 is one of those Bible verses that can change everything for us if we really believe it. It can eliminate comparison. It says, "So God created mankind in his own image, in the image of God he created them; male and female he created them."

This verse means that we are made in the very image of the One who is without rival and without equal. When we compare and compete with one another, we are essentially attacking part of the image of God in each other. Every person God made offers a sneak peek at the goodness of God. Right now there are more than seven billion people on earth, *and each one bears something of the image of God.*

Instead of letting that phenomenal truth take our breath away, we compare. We become jealous. We drag each other down. I think a much better idea would be to appreciate what we see in one another and to celebrate the aspects of God's image in other people instead of competing with them—because He has no rival and no equal.

I want to encourage you and remind you that you are one of a kind. There's no one else on earth like you. There is something of the image of God in you. Comparison is a tool of the Enemy; it's not of God. So the next time you feel tempted to compare yourself to someone else, tell yourself that both of you are valued, needed, and special. What's good about the other person is not a threat to you; it's something you can use to build that person up.

I hope and pray that you and I, and all believers, will become the kind of people Paul wrote about in 1 Thessalonians. Someday soon, maybe we'll be able to say we're continuing to "encourage one another and build each other up, just as in fact [we] are doing."

You can easily enough see how this kind of thing works by looking no further than your own body. Your body has many parts—limbs, organs, cells—but no matter how many parts you can name, you're still one body. It's exactly the same with Christ. . . . I want you to think about how all this makes you more significant, not less. A body isn't just a single part blown up into something huge. It's all the different-but-similar parts arranged and functioning together. If Foot said, "I'm not elegant like Hand, embellished with rings; I guess I don't belong to this body," would that make it so? If Ear said, "I'm not beautiful like Eye, limpid and expressive; I don't deserve a place on the head," would you want to remove it from the body? If the body was all eye, how could it hear? If all ear, how could it smell? As it is, we see that God has carefully placed each part of the body right where he wanted it. . . . The way God designed our bodies is a model for understanding our lives together as a church: every part dependent on every other part, the parts we mention and the parts we don't, the parts we see and the parts we don't. If one part hurts, every other part is involved in the hurt, and in the healing. If one part flourishes, every other part enters into the exuberance.

—1 CORINTHIANS 12:12, 14–18, 25–26 MSG

Where Confidence Comes From

WOULD YOU AGREE WITH ME THAT THE WORLD PUTS A LOT of pressure on people? For real. Just think about how hard the world tries to tell us who we should be, how we should look, what we should say, how we should vote, what we should approve of, who we should admire, and on and on. There aren't many parts of our lives the world doesn't try to influence. More and more, it attempts to entice us to put our confidence and trust in these things. It feels to me like shaky ground.

I don't know about you, but I am thinking, *Where is the stability in that?* The world is ever changing. I can't count on worldly wisdom to help me make good decisions. I can't look to the world's standards of beauty—because they change every time a new blog goes up or a new magazine comes out. And I definitely wouldn't want to build my life on this ever-changing value system.

I often think many of us are following the same handbook for life, but no one has a copy of it. We can't hold it in our hands and read it, but we know exactly what it says. It's an unwritten set of guidelines about how to thrive and be successful in life, and its author is "The World." It goes something like, "Look out for number one." "You do you." "You only live once." "Wear less to get more." "Whatever it takes to get likes." I have to ask, Does anyone actually like the outcome? Are we happy doing what the handbook instructs?

It's as if everyone is following the same diet but nobody's losing weight. If that happened to you, would you keep eating according to the plan? No! Anytime we do something and we don't see results, we stop. That's just common sense.

The world's handbook for living is like an ineffective diet. It's not helpful. It doesn't take us where we need to go. The results it gives us leave us feeling hungry for something else. In fact, I can't think of anything valuable in it. Nothing about it will remain or enable us to stand. It's totally unreliable.

Even though the world in Paul's day was different than ours, the problem was the same. He wrote this passage to the church in Rome:

> Do not be conformed to this world [any longer with its superficial values and customs], but be transformed and progressively changed [as you mature spiritually] by the renewing of your mind [focusing on godly values and ethical attitudes], so that you may prove [for yourselves] what the will of God is, that which is good and acceptable and perfect [in His plan and purpose for you]. (Romans 12:2 AMP)

Wow. These words will give us life and set us free. Paul told us exactly how to live. He said we are not to be "conformed to this world," which goes much further than simply saying, "Don't pay attention to it." He understood how hard the world works to influence us and said, "Don't let that happen." Why? Because the world has "superficial values and customs." In other words, it has no depth and no strength. When you look below the surface of these superficial values and customs—our social media presence, chasing after money or fame or popularity—we don't find anything that sustains us or has lasting value. Unfortunately, so many times we continue in them, hoping that we'll eventually feel fulfilled. Jim Carrey famously summed this up so clearly when he said, "I think everybody should get rich and famous and do everything they ever dreamed of so they can see it's not the answer."[23] How many celebrities have you

WE CAN PLACE OUR
CONFIDENCE IN GOD AND
TRULY LIVE ROOTED IN HIS
NEVER-CHANGING LOVE.

seen who seem to have it all but are unhappy, lonely, or addicted to drugs or alcohol? Yet we still look to them as our idols and wish we had what they had. For the path to life and true fulfillment, we have to set our minds on things that last.

I know from experience that a ton of people can know your name and you can have a lot of followers yet still feel alone. On social media, it's easy to make ourselves look like we are living loud and large, but we aren't. Think again about the prodigal son. The brother who stayed home may have thought his younger brother was thriving and having fun, but in reality his life was lonely and miserable.

> We have to set our minds on things that last.

We need to live in our reality, not in the images we try to present. Yet trying to live a life that mimics our posts and profiles is epidemic. Almost everyone is doing it. And you know what? Underneath the filters and the captions, everyone feels the same way. There's still an isolation that haunts our generation. The results of it are scary—anxiety, stress, depression, perfectionism, performance mentality, temporary highs, and mental illness. Likes will never fill you up. When the temporary high goes away, it leaves behind a feeling of emptiness.

Our outward appearance, a picture with a great filter, more "likes" than the photo we posted last week, enough compliments in a comment section to make us feel sufficiently approved of—these things will never give us the same confidence God can give us. They won't even come close.

If we choose to spend our first moments every morning facing God instead of scrolling through social media, we will begin to find our security, comfort, meaning, purpose, and confidence in Him. Remember, when we spend our time trying to measure up, striving to paint a picture of ourselves in order to feel accepted or to impress others or to be liked, we will always feel empty. That's the world's way to live. But when we fill ourselves with eternal truth that we can stand on forever, we will walk taller, live more boldly, and be steadfast in the knowledge of who we are because of who God is in us. We will rest in His love for us with the knowledge that His love doesn't change based on if we are picture-perfect. Our bold confidence will come solely from Him and not from things of this world. We don't have to be conformed to this world and let it toss us up and down with every new trend and idea. Instead, we can place our confidence in Him and truly live rooted in His never-changing love.

If we are constantly changing our routines or mind-sets to match the pattern of the world, we will be swayed by every new idea, trend, value, or emotion. We will never be rooted or grounded firmly in anything. The things of this world change daily. We can't count on it.

Confidence comes from knowing you can put your trust in something and *it will never let you down*. The only safe, solid place to put your trust is in God.

One of my favorite Bible stories is about a young man named Daniel and his three friends, Shadrach, Meshach, and Abednego. Daniel and his friends knew exactly where to put their confidence. They did not conform to what everyone else was doing; they never wavered, no matter how much pressure the world put on them—even if the pressure came from a rich and powerful king.

In Daniel 1, a king named Nebuchadnezzar was looking for men from Israel to serve in his kingdom in Babylon. He wanted men who were young and handsome, wise, intelligent, discerning, quick to understand, and able to serve him well. The king assigned a daily portion for their meals—the finest food, along with the wine he himself drank.

But there was a problem with the elaborate feasts the king provided. Daniel, Shadrach, Meshach, and Abednego followed the Torah (the Jewish law in Bible times), and the food they were required to eat went against the law of God at the time. In order to walk in obedience to God, these men decided to drink only water and eat only vegetables.

For ten days, they ate this way. Soon others noticed a change in their outward appearance. Daniel, Shadrach, Meshach, and Abednego looked better and were healthier than any of the other men in the kingdom. God gave these four men knowledge, skills in different kinds of languages, and wisdom. In addition, God gave Daniel the ability to understand visions and dreams. This favor from the Lord made Daniel and his friends valuable in the kingdom. Instead of being punished for not eating the king's food, they were given special privileges.

Daniel remained steadfast in his faith, and God responded with an amazing display of faithfulness. The faithfulness Daniel experienced established his confident trust in God. Instead of trying to feel confident because of his outward appearance and physical strength or mental sharpness, which would have been valuable to an earthly kingdom, Daniel determined to truly find confidence in God, trusting that He would come through for him.

You can trust God completely.

Daniel walked in a confidence that was different than the superficial confidence of the people around him. Their confidence would eventually crumble, but Daniel's would stand strong under pressure. He knew what was within him and understood that confidence is an inside job, not something that comes from anything external. He had seen God's faithfulness, and he knew he could trust Him completely.

From Liked
to Loved

WHEN I SPEAK PUBLICLY ABOUT CONFIDENCE, SOMETIMES I sense people getting uncomfortable. When people hear that confidence is about what's inside of them rather than anything on the outside, it presses on something in their hearts. Maybe it's pressing on something for you right now. Maybe you are thinking, *Whoa. I really struggle with confidence. I have tried so many things to help me become more confident, but it hasn't done anything except give me a temporary boost. I haven't found anything that offers me the deep and lasting confidence I'm hungry for.* If that sounds like something you've thought, keep reading. I've got good news for you. The truth is, you're just one perspective change away: it's as simple as moving from being liked to being loved.

You may be thinking, *Wait a minute, Sadie. Isn't everything in our world today about being liked?* Let me explain.

You know what it's like when you are in the beginning stages of dating someone. When you see that person, it makes you excited about life, and you want to present your very best self. You make sure that every time he is around, you look good and smell good. I know that's the way I felt when I first met Christian. I wish I were kidding when I say that every time Christian came to see me, I got a spray tan. He is from Florida and is sun-kissed, so I was thinking that if I wanted to be kissed myself, I needed to go for the spray. You best believe I was pulling out the A game for him!

> Take a deep breath, and be confident, seen, known, and loved.

Once I realized I really liked him, I felt like I had to keep up this image I had created. The funny thing is, I am never like this. I'm not typically the person who cares about what I look like, but I really wanted him to like me. He had his own way of wanting me to like him. He took me to the best date spots and bought me sweet surprises. I mean he went all out; he surprised me left and right.

These stories unfold differently for everyone, but for us, after about four months of dating, our "I like you" became "I like you so much," which led to "I like you sooooo much." Then we got really creative: "I like you so much it's crazy!" And then, "I like you some kind of crazy!"

But no matter how many ways we communicated how much we liked each other, something was missing. That's because "I like you" doesn't stick. There's no real commitment to it, and you cannot find much confidence or rest in it.

But I will never forget the minute he said, "I love you." I mean, the instant you say "I love you," everything changes. You can take a deep breath and be confident, seen, known, and loved.

To show me he liked me, he gave me a million over-the-top surprises when we looked our best and felt our best, but on November 20, 2018, when I woke up from having fallen asleep on his shoulder during a movie, he looked at me with my messy hair and my tired eyes and said, "I love you."

After I knew I was loved, I worried less about how I looked. Our primary date destination for celebrating fun days became Waffle House. I felt freer to be silly as we rode in the car together. I wasn't striving to be liked anymore because I could relax in knowing I was loved.

I believe that our generation is in the "I like you" season. Our entire mind-set—our only goal, oftentimes—is to be liked. Think about social media. What was meant to connect people has for so many become a battlefield of comparison and competition. And for what? Likes. The competition and comparison are even internal. We look at our number of "likes" to see if people liked us better in the swimsuit photos or when we were skinnier or when we were with a certain person. All this mental energy creates pressure and crafts a false image of perfection we feel we have to obtain in order to be liked.

One definition of *like* is to "find agreeable, enjoyable, or satisfactory."[24] The social media definition of like is "to win one's approval." Do you see how neither of these definitions are ultimately sustainable?

I've been thinking about why we try to settle for just being liked instead of diving into love, and I think there are a few reasons. First is the instant gratification that comes from being "liked." Dopamine is one of the brain's transmitters that contributes to feelings of pleasure and satisfaction. It is associated with food, exercise, love, sex, gambling, drugs, and now social media. It feels good to be liked, but that feeling doesn't last, so we need another hit.

Love requires vulnerability, authenticity, work, and sacrifice.

The second reason I believe we prefer likes over love is a fear of commitment. Okay, maybe you don't want to admit to an all-out fear, but at the very least there seems to be a reluctance to commit in the world today. Not many people these days want to truly commit to anything. A common conversation goes like this: "Are you dating?" "No, just talking!" We are reluctant to commit, and love is a commitment.

We want to flirt. We want to interact on social media. We want to be "talking to" people. We want instant satisfaction. But love requires vulnerability, authenticity, work, and sacrifice. It's not a quick hit; it's a long-term commitment.

I believe we aren't only keeping others in the "like" zone; we are treating our relationship with Jesus the same way. Following Jesus is not like following someone on social media. You cannot just click a button and like Him when you agree with what He says, then unfollow Him when you disagree. That is not how a relationship of love works. Love is a commitment and an action. You have to dive all in. But love is where you find security, where you don't have to show your perfect self every day. People like you when you are "agreeable, enjoyable, or satisfactory." But God's Word tells us that "God demonstrates his own love for us in this: While we were still sinners, Christ died for us" (Romans 5:8). I'd say that's a little bit better than just being liked.

> Love is a commitment and an action.

Tell the Lions to Shut Their Mouths

I MENTIONED EARLIER THAT THE STORY OF DANIEL IS ONE OF my favorites because he truly knew how to remain and reside in God, and his confidence was firmly rooted in Him, which we read about in Daniel 1. I also like his story because of what happens in Daniel 6.

By the time we get to chapter 6, Daniel had distinguished himself so much that King Darius appointed Daniel as one of three administrators in the kingdom. Before long, the king decided to put Daniel in a position of leadership over the entire kingdom (vv. 1–3). Some of the other leaders did not like that, and they plotted against Daniel. The problem was, they could not justly accuse him of anything wrong, so they set him up (haters gonna hate) (vv. 4–5).

They went to the king and suggested that he decree that everyone in the kingdom had to pray to him or risk being thrown into a den of hungry lions. The men knew Daniel would never pray to King Darius because he was so devoted to the God of Israel. They knew it so well that they asked the king to put his decree in writing so it could not be changed (vv. 8–9).

As soon as Daniel heard about the decree, he had an anxiety attack. His mouth went dry. His knees went weak. Cue the dramatic music because *he could not handle it,* right? Wrong! That's probably how I would have felt, but it's not at all what happened to Daniel. He went to his room and prayed to the Lord *with the windows open*—where everyone could hear him (v. 10). When the men caught him praying, they told the king. Although King Darius wanted to spare Daniel's life, he felt he could not go back on his decree, so he ordered Daniel into the lions' den.

God, had He wanted to, could have saved Daniel immediately. He could have given him the same kind of strength He gave David to kill a lion and a bear with his bare hands (1 Samuel 17:34–36). But that was not what God had in mind.

Just before Daniel was thrown into the den, King Darius said, "May your God, whom you constantly serve, rescue you Himself!" (Daniel 6:16 AMP). God chose to send an angel to shut the lions' mouths. He did not merely rescue Daniel's life; it was also His response to the king's cry to prove that He is God and He does show up. When the king saw that Daniel had been saved, he declared the greatness of Daniel's God to the whole land and decreed that He should be revered.

Daniel was thrown in the lions' den and faced the beasts, but the chapter does not start and end with Daniel; it starts and ends with King Darius. I believe the message of Daniel 6 is about a king's life and heart being changed so that he can then change a kingdom.

Let's stop and think about this. You may have heard about Daniel and the lions' den before. And you may have been told that Daniel is the hero of the story, the ultimate brave guy, one of the great spiritual giants and prayer warriors of all time, the poster child for confidence in God. And he is. You'd be exactly right to view him that way. I don't think anyone knows better than Daniel about that feeling I got when I was skydiving—that when you face your greatest fear, you experience the greatest freedom. I don't think it could get any scarier than sitting in a den, in the dark, filled with lions. Can you imagine the freedom and joy he felt when God closed the mouths of the lions and that door was opened the next morning?

Daniel is amazing. His faith inspires me. We can learn great lessons from his life and use them to help us grow spiritually. But again, chapter 6 isn't really about him. It's about the king.

That hit me like a bolt of lightning while I was reading this story one day. I love that about God. We can walk with Him for a long time and believe what we've been taught for years; then one day He shows us a different perspective. He teaches us a new lesson from an old story. That's what I want us to see together in Daniel 6.

We look for lessons in the Bible to help us. We approach them, asking, "What can I learn?" or "How can I apply this story?" Sometimes they challenge us to look at the supporting actors, not just the main characters.

> When you face your greatest fear, you experience the greatest freedom.

In chapter 6, Daniel did not do anything spectacular or slay any giants. Daniel's way of fighting this battle was to be willing to fall on his knees and pray. He was righteous. He was bold. He humbled himself and let almighty God do what almighty God does—and

DON'T LET
THE LIONS
STOP YOU
FROM LIVING.
FACE THEM
WITH FAITH.

that is more powerful than anything he could have imagined. Then Daniel and his God were honored everywhere among all people because "humility comes before honor" (Proverbs 18:12). Daniel was not the hero of this story; God was the hero. But without Daniel's confident faith, the king would not have been able to witness the heroic act of God.

You don't have to be a speaker, a preacher, or someone famous on Instagram for God to use you. You can be in the lions' den, and your life can make a difference—because it's not about what you can do for yourself; it's about what the power of heaven can do through you. Notice that all Daniel did was trust God, and God sent an angel to do the rest. You may be fighting and clawing some lions in your life, trying to silence them yourself when you really only need to be still and allow God to send an angel to shut their mouths.

I firmly believe God still sends angels into human situations. They protect; they lead; they bring good news; they rescue; they are heaven's army; and they come only at God's command. When we choose to trust God, as Daniel did, God's angels are there for us too.

From the world's perspective, there may be times when we appear to be in the wrong place at the wrong time. Maybe things just aren't working out for us, or maybe we feel we are the ones in the lions' den, meaning that we feel we're being attacked. But from heaven's viewpoint, we might just be right where we need to be. We don't have to submit to the world's storyline of fear and anxiety. We can rise to heaven's perspective and put our trust in God, who has an army of angels at His disposal.

Even though you and I are living in dark times, I highly doubt any of us will have to stare a lion in the face as Daniel did. For me, the lions represent fear. In the darkness of the den, Daniel probably could not see the lions, but he felt the danger around him. Similarly, you may not be able to see what is threatening you, but you feel the power of the fear that comes with it. Have confidence in God. Stop believing in the power of the lions and believe instead in the power of God. Stop worrying about the danger and start trusting in Him. Maybe there's someone like the king in your story, who will see you prevail and give glory to God.

I truly believe that if we—in our generation—start living like Daniel, we will see God move for us like He did in Daniel's day.

I wrote a lot about my own personal lions I've had to stare down in my book *Live Fearless*. Anything that threatens you and is out of your control can be a lion. Lions can appear to you in different ways—people's rude opinions, conflicts in friendship, divorces, someone cheating on you, unhealthy relationships, natural disasters, sicknesses, moves, or unexpected life changes. Lions are a part of life. It is important, though, that we do not let the lions stop us from living but that we face them with faith.

When we face things that threaten our lives, the only place we can find peace is in the One who conquered death and is the giver of life. Isaiah 54:17 says that no weapon forged against us shall prosper. This might be confusing because you may have witnessed things in life that cause pain or even death to those around you. You may wonder how this verse makes sense. To fully live, we have to acknowledge death but know that Jesus is victorious even in death. God did not just give you life on this earth; He sent Jesus to give you eternal life. John 3:16 says, "For this is how God loved the world: He gave his one and only Son, so that everyone who believes in him will not perish but have eternal life" (NLT). Face your lions with this kind of faith, with the knowledge that they have no power over the One who gives eternal life.

Believe, Belong, Become

A FEW YEARS AGO, WE RAISED ENOUGH MONEY ON THE LIVE Original tour to build a safe house in Peru with a great organization called Help One Now. It's a place for girls rescued from trafficking. My family and friends and I went to see the house, and it is amazing.

While we were traveling in Peru, we explored a little bit. We saw Machu Picchu, which was incredible. We even got to hug a sloth—a lifetime dream for me, believe it or not. It was the best hug I had ever had. After that, I thought, *When a man hugs me like that sloth did, I'll know he is the one!* This was before I met Christian, of course.

During our trip, we also decided to visit the Amazon River, and this is where things got serious. I was genuinely shocked by what

I saw. There was trash everywhere, to the point that every step I took landed on a piece of trash. We saw people using the river as a bathroom; other people were washing their clothes in it and even bathing in its waters. The river was flooded with trash and flooded with people who were trying to make it feel like home. Some of them had used whatever materials they could find to build little houses for themselves by hand.

As I stood and looked around, trying to take in such a sight, I heard some noise in the distance. As I looked in the direction of the sound, I saw a lot of tiny heads peeking over at me. I smiled and waved from afar. Then one brave little girl took off running as fast as she could and jumped in my arms. I started to play with her hair and tickle her arm. By the look on her face and the easy way she relaxed her shoulders, I could tell that she was enjoying having someone show her that kind of fun and affection. Her name was Arianna, and her bravery caused several more children to run to me until we were all tickling and giggling.

The organization's local leader took us to the Amazon that day and told me something that stuck with me: she said I would never know how just that one touch could change the trajectory of that little girl's life. Just the feeling of love, she said, could make a bigger difference than I could imagine. She shared with us that the diseases in that region are so bad and the malnutrition is so horrible that life expectancy is very low. The people who live in

> If you believe you belong in God's family, then you can become all He created you to be.

this area have very little hope that they will ever get out of these circumstances, so their mind-set tends to be, "Well, if we are going to die young, we might as well do what we want."

If you have never seen this part of the Amazon, I can tell you that it is a place of beauty polluted by trafficking, drunkenness, and abuse. The riverbed is hidden by trash and desperation.

When we left the river that day, my brother John Luke also said something I will never forget. "If you grew up living in trash," he reflected, "it would be hard to not begin to believe that you are trash."

I once prepared a message called "Belong, Believe, Become." I almost preached those three verbs in that order until I became aware of stories like Arianna's.

But I had to switch those first two around. If you *believe* you *belong* in a certain space, you will likely *become* what is expected of you. But with one touch of hope, your life can be changed. Maybe as you have lived your life with other people, others have spoken things over you that feel like pollution—things that make you think you're not worth much more than the trash on the riverbed, things that take away your hope and your desire to truly live. But if you believe you belong in God's family, then you can become all He created you to be, like in the story of a friend I met in Somalia.

I was in Mogadishu, which is known to be the world's most dangerous place, when I met one of the sweetest souls in the world. He used to be a child soldier.

Trust me, it's as shocking as it sounds. All I could think was, *Like what?*

This seventeen-year-old's story wrecked my world. He had one of the brightest, most genuine smiles I have ever seen. I never could have imagined his life story would be what it is. As a young boy, he was recruited into an African terrorist group. Sadly, this is a reality for many teens like him in countries that are ravaged by war. Some are kidnapped; some are sold by their families. Others join because of the promise of food, money, and schooling for themselves and their siblings. I don't know the full story behind why he got there, but I know this: at seven-

> There is power in getting past what you believe *about* someone to what you believe *for* them.

teen he had seen more than any person should ever have to see. He had reached a point when they asked him to murder his uncle. His dad received word of the mission his son was on and faked his mother's death to try to get him to come home. When he came running home, his parents had the police arrest him, stating that he was a terrorist—even though he was just a kid.

The young man was thrown into prison and abused in every way. After some time, author and speaker Bob Goff and his organization, Love Does, went into the prisons in Somalia to try to rescue any child soldiers under the age of eighteen and to seek justice on this issue. Bob shared with me that this young man was one of the toughest to get released because while the boy was in prison and during the attempt to rescue him, the young man's dad would visit the prison and tell the guards and the judge not to let his son go. He would tell them that his son belonged to a terrorist group and that he believed the boy would harm their family.

This went on for a while. Then, Bob told me, one day the dad showed up and completely softened his heart. He told his son that he believed the best in him and that he wanted the best for him. Bob said not long after that the young man became the bright-smiling seventeen-year-old kid I met surfing. Yes, you read that right—surfing. One of the things we were able to do on this trip was a therapy surfing program with the young men who had been brought out of African terrorist groups.

While we were out in the water, I asked the young man what he wanted to do in life, and he said, "I want to travel around Africa and share Jesus." Remember when we talked about the power of getting past what you believe *about* someone to what you believe *for* them? This is the belief *for* someone on full display!

If you believe you belong to a terrorist group, then you will take actions to become just that—and if the people around you keep speaking over you what they believe you to be, you will have a much harder time feeling that you could be anything different. What I love about this young man's story is that it just took a father's words of belief and affirmation to forever change the trajectory of his life. You see, once you feel as though you belong to something more and begin to believe that for yourself, then you can become whatever that is.

Mark 5:25–34 tells the story of a woman some Bible translations refer to as the woman with "an issue of blood." The "issue" meant that the bleeding could not be stopped, but it was also "an issue" as we think of an issue today—a problem. She had been bleeding for twelve years, and at that time she would have been viewed as unclean. No one would have been willing to touch her or to even be near her.

> Jesus gave her the freedom to become all that she could be.

One day this woman heard that a man named Jesus was making His way through her town. Because of the things she had heard, she thought, *If I could just touch His clothes, then maybe I could be healed.*

Determined and desperate, she pressed through the crowd that day. She probably had to push herself past people's condescending looks and stares, most likely feeling she did not belong and was not wanted. But when she got close to Jesus, she stretched out her hand and touched His cloak. And she was healed immediately.

The story says that "at once" Jesus stopped and asked who touched Him (Mark 5:30). It seemed funny to the disciples around Him that Jesus would ask such a question because so many people were gathered in the crowd that day. But Jesus asked again.

The woman went to Him, trembling in fear, dreading the attention, and not wanting those who knew her for her issue to see her in the crowd. What He spoke over the woman next was the very first time we get to experience God saying this word through the mouth of Jesus: "Daughter" (Mark 5:34).

I can imagine her feeling an immediate sense of belonging to something bigger than herself. Just think about that for a moment, how life-changing it must have been for her.

Then Jesus said, "Your faith has healed you" (Mark 5:34). What was her faith? She believed that an encounter with Jesus could change her life, and what she believed led to her testimony. It changed the trajectory of her life.

Jesus went on to say, "Go in peace and be freed from your suffering" (Mark 5:34). He gave her the freedom to become all that she could be.

A touch and a word from Jesus can change everything about your life. Do not settle for what it looks like right now or for what others believe about you or for what may have been spoken over you. There is life and hope in the promises of God.

Stay Until the Story Gets Good

I N HIGH SCHOOL I WAS GOOD AT THROWING THE JAVELIN AND shot put, so the track and field coach asked me to join the team. "Okay," I told him. "But I can't run."

He said, "Okay. You can just do field events." So we had a deal.

Track and field is a team sport, but the scores are based on individual performances. For each performance, athletes are awarded a certain number of points, which go toward the team total. The better each individual does, the more points the team gets.

As our team prepared for our regional meet, the coach gathered all of us and said, "We need as many points as possible in the regionals, so some of you will have to compete in events you don't normally do. We're going to have to have someone run the two-mile."

As soon as I heard that, I tried to hide behind the people in front of me—like you do when you don't want someone to call on you in class. I was so clearly not a runner, no one would think I would have been in danger of being called on. I was happy in the field events and felt confident I could do them well. I was not interested in doing anything else, *especially* the two-mile.

Now, I know some of you reading this book get up at 5:00 in the morning and drink juice the same color as the grass you run on. And you are laughing about my two-mile crisis. But two miles was more than I had ever tried to run around a track.

> Life gets hard,
> but it is always
> worth the run.

As my mind went back and forth from *no way* to *no way*, I suddenly heard the coach say, "Sadie, you'll do the two-mile."

Everyone on the team started laughing, including me (at first), because I thought he was joking. We all knew I would not do well in a two-mile event.

He responded, "Why is that funny?"

When an authority figure wants to know why something is funny, what you thought was hilarious just moments before is no longer funny.

Just a couple of days later I was lined up on the track. As soon as the race started, I knew it would not end well for me. It wasn't long before everyone in the event lapped me. Even the middle schooler who was competing in the high school meet passed me.

The coach must have realized how terrible the experience was for me because as I rounded the corner where he was standing, he yelled, "Sadie, do not step off this track. You are going to finish this race!"

I was miserable—*so* miserable and *so* dramatic. I remember looking up at the beaming sun and clouds and saying as I rounded

SINCE WE ARE SURROUNDED BY SUCH A HUGE CROWD OF WITNESSES TO THE LIFE OF FAITH, LET US STRIP OFF EVERY WEIGHT THAT SLOWS US DOWN, ESPECIALLY THE SIN THAT SO EASILY TRIPS US UP. AND LET US RUN WITH ENDURANCE THE RACE GOD HAS SET BEFORE US.

—HEBREWS 12:1 NLT

the sixth lap, "Oh, God, I have lived a good life, but take me now—or come down from heaven!" The humiliation of being lapped by literally everyone else in the race was bad enough. But even worse was the revelation that I would have to run the last lap all alone, with all the spectators watching me struggle to put one foot in front of the other.

Suddenly, out of the corner of my eye, I saw someone running down the bleachers toward the track, and I heard the first lines of my warm-up song for basketball. My brother John Luke was headed straight for me with the song playing on his phone. He had come down from the bleachers to run that last lap with me! The spectators loved it! I loved it! Everyone who had felt sorry for me minutes earlier had re-engaged and stood to cheer us on. It was not a pity clap; it was an uproar. They were pumped up because they saw something that day that amazed them—my brother completely took away the humiliation of my performance.

> Keep running your race.

What John Luke did for me that day was a perfect picture of what Jesus does for us all the time. He meets us in the place of our embarrassment and failure and redeems our story. He makes a pitiful picture into a beautiful, powerful visual we could never have created for ourselves.

If you are feeling humiliated for some reason right now, I want to encourage you. You may even be past the feeling of humiliation and feel you would rather die than face the last lap in front of you, but friend, *keep running your race*. Don't stop when it gets hard or even when the middle schooler leaves you in the dust. Don't let the most painful part of the story become the end of it. Keep moving ahead, even if you have to go slowly, trusting Jesus to redeem everything.

The apostle Paul wrote about this, saying, "I press on to reach the end of the race and receive the heavenly prize for which God, through Christ Jesus, is calling us" (Philippians 3:14 NLT). That's pretty impressive when we think about everything he went through—being thrown in prison, being whipped, facing death several times, being beaten with rods three times, being stoned once, and being shipwrecked three times (2 Corinthians 11:23–25). No matter what he had to endure, Paul never gave up.

Life is like a race. It takes humility to keep running when you feel the race will never end, but that's exactly what God calls us to do. I don't have much in common with Paul; I've never been beaten or shipwrecked, but I do know what it's like to run a race that feels impossible to finish, and I am not just referring to that two miles. Life gets hard, but it is always worth the run. There are a lot of people who are watching and are impacted by your continuing to run, no matter how insignificant it may feel.

One reason you are living is that God wants to give you a story, a testimony that helps the world see who He is. Jesus trusts us with our stories. I think that is amazing to think about. Yet sometimes we try to bail right before our story gets good because that is usually when we get pushed beyond the limits of our comfort. Life becomes hard. Someone lets us down. Something we were really hoping for does not happen. A friend rejects us. All kinds of things happen to cause pain and disappointment, and sometimes they hurt so much that we just want to quit. However, it is so important that we keep pressing on because that decision to push past the pain and the fear will change everything for your life and will impact a lot of people around you. You see, if we don't press through the hard times, then the hard times will be all we'll know and all that others see in our lives. But if we push through them in the power of the Holy Spirit—God within you—we get to the good stuff. The difficulties make us stronger and our stories better. They are part of the way God transforms us, and our transformation is what leads to our testimonies.

> The difficulties make us stronger and our stories better.

A Letter to My Sisters and Friends

M Y SISTERS ARE SOME OF THE CLOSEST PEOPLE TO ME, and my friends sometimes feel as close as sisters. They are some of the biggest blessings in my life. After we've talked so much about finding life wherever you are, I want to share with you some advice I would give my sisters and my friends from lessons I learned over the past few years. Some of these lessons I've learned the hard way. And because I consider you my friend too, I'd love it if you didn't have to go through all that. If I can write to you as a sister and a friend and spare you that—not to mention saving you some time, drama, and emotion—the challenges of my journey will be worth it.

At some point in this book, we've touched on every single one of these lessons because they're key in finding life. Now I want to speak directly into your life, to encourage you forward.

LET'S TALK ABOUT CONFIDENCE

When it comes to your confidence, it's important to realize that there is nothing you could have—and nothing you ever will have—that will make you a more confident person than you are now. Your confidence is nothing more than a choice to believe in the originality of who God formed you to be when He knit you together in your mother's womb. Hear me again: your confidence is a choice. Choose to be confident in who you are right now, in where you are right now, and most importantly in who God is now and forever. He will always remind you of who you are. Do not look to the left or right at your sisters and compare. God did not compare them to you when He created you, so your comparison will only bring forth things that are not of Him. Comparison is a tactic of the Enemy. It attempts to steal your confidence and bring about jealousy and insecurity.

Remember: you are strong. I believe that everything God has put in you is exactly what the world needs for such a time as this. His perfect love for you will eliminate any fear as He sends you out into the world. Rise up to that call.

> Remember: you are strong.

When things get scary, that is when your confidence in Him will really come into play. You need to already know who He is so that you can be still, lock eyes with Him, and know that He has you. Things will happen during your lifetime that will cause fear to flare up in you, and they will come in many forms. But, my sister and my friend, take heart; He will always be fighting on your behalf. Remember He sees it all, and He is in control of it all. He is for you, not against you.

When you find yourself afraid, everything in you will want to run away from the fear, but I challenge you to run to it. When you see that the very place that fear is found is the place where fear will be conquered, it will build your confident trust in the Lord. Be encouraged by what God did for Moses, Joshua, and Daniel. Be strengthened as you think about what He has done for your friends and family members, and even what He has done for you time and time again.

> God can make problems into good things.

When you let God lead, you might find yourself in some rather scary places, but remain steadfast in Him and stay confident that He will bring provision and fight on your behalf. It's in those times that miracles happen and nations change. One way to describe fear is that it is the belief that something is a threat to you and will bring forth harm. Right now, instead of believing in fear, believe in faith and know that no weapon formed against you shall prosper. Nothing is a threat to the mighty hand of God.

WHEN THINGS IN LIFE CHANGE

When nothing feels constant in your life, God is the only thing that will remain the same. People will come and go, but He will be around forever, and there is not one thing you can do to change that. He will send His angels on your behalf to encamp around you. Even when you might sometimes feel alone and anxiety begins to stir in your heart, remember that you are never truly alone. He will consistently be there.

WHEN YOU DO NOT KNOW TRUTH FROM A LIE

You will face choices and temptations. The Enemy's plan is not original. He has worked it since the first humans were created—Adam and Eve. The Enemy will make you question what you know God says about you—like the fact that you are "fearfully and wonderfully made" (Psalm 139:14), that He has a plan to "give you hope and a future" (Jeremiah 29:11), and the other promises He makes to you in His Word. That's why it is very important that you remind yourself of the truth and recognize the lies.

> God can make problems into good things.

Otherwise, truth and lies will begin to blend together, and you will find yourself in a place where you were never meant to be.

Always remember that what the Enemy means for evil, God can make into good. Look at some of the things you are insecure about right now and stare them down. Yeah, that. That very thing that seems so huge or so difficult or so scary may just be the thing God wants to use as your weapon of strength. Just shift your lens. Choose to no longer look at that thing as the problem in your life; view it as potential—potential God wants to make into something good. In order to see that, you have to know Scripture and know God. Start reading His Word and filling your mind with it so that you can believe it and start speaking it.

WHEN YOU DO NOT KNOW WHERE TO GO NEXT

When you don't know where to go next, let God's peace lead you. There will be moments when you cannot see the way forward and you have no idea what to do. In those times, you will have to trust.

Know that God's peace will always meet you at every destination. His love knows no end. God will provide what you need in every season, and He will match the pure desires of your heart. Be open minded. What you think you need may not be best for where He is taking you. What He will give will be what sets you apart for the purpose He has been waiting to reveal in you.

WHEN LOVE HAS HURT YOU

I want to tell you to not give up on love. I am sorry if you have heard the world throw out the word *love* when it wasn't real or when it was not the way God meant it to be and it has hurt you and made you afraid of being known and afraid to step into relationships. I want you to

know that God is the Redeemer. He is the Creator, and He is the very essence of what love is. When you experience the love He has created, you will experience freedom, you will fully be yourself, you will be fully known, and fear will be far away.

On this side of heaven, perfect love is found only in God our Father. People are flawed; sometimes we hurt one another and have to ask for forgiveness, but be encouraged that love is real and that those who know God know love. We can be made more perfect in His love.

I have learned so much as I have read about how Jacob pursued Rachel in Genesis 29:1–30. Wait for that kind of love. You deserve someone who will wait for you, someone who will pursue you.

Also, in a dating relationship, don't spend time fighting over the things that *might* happen in the future; that is a tactic the Enemy will use to steal your present time. I regret the years of arguing over a future that never even came to be. The truth is, you don't know the future, and God's Word tells us not to worry about tomorrow, that it will take care of itself (Matthew 6:34). Be in the present, experience God's perfect love, and don't give up on loving His people.

Don't give up on love.

WHEN IT COMES TO BEAUTY

Have you ever looked in the mirror and didn't find anything beautiful? You may not recognize beauty in the mirror every day, because beauty is not what you've been looking for. That's why you have been missing it. You were looking for an image the world gave you and told you was beautiful, and you limited the definition of beauty to the world's standard.

There's a trick involved in the world's definition of beauty. It sets an unrealistic standard that is designed to provoke comparison and competition. It's intended to cause you to think you always need more or less of something to meet the standard. It will send you on a journey, but you will never really reach the standard because there is not a realistic image to achieve. Trends will always keep you feeling like you've just missed them. If you hold too tightly to the world's standards of beauty, you will never feel beautiful. It's set up

YOUR CONFIDENCE

IS A CHOICE.

to always make you feel not quite there because it's not real, and it wasn't God's design.

When God created you, He created a work of art, a masterpiece not meant to be compared to any other form of creation. The image of beauty you were designed to reach is right in front of you. In you He has created a new, original design for the world to enjoy beholding. Go look around, and you will not find one other piece of creation that looks exactly like you.

I hope these words remind you of what beauty is. You are beautiful because you were created in the image of God. There is no one else like you. Who you were made to be is more than enough for what this world needs. You were born lacking no good thing, so never feel the urge to strive for it.

Now, sisters and friends, I want you to do something. Go look in the mirror. Take off any worldly lens that has affected the way you see yourself—a lens of insecurity, jealousy, comparison, negativity, self-hatred, or anything else. And stare at yourself.

You are altogether beautiful, my darling.

Wow, the Lord takes such great delight in you.

Look at the color of your eyes. Look at the strands of your hair and the unique shapes and features of your face. God made you, and you are exactly how He intended you to be. He created every detail—details no other person on the earth has. He did this so He could reveal a new image of beauty and another side of Himself to the world.

On this day, choose for the rest of your life to turn your eyes away from the standard of what is "supposed" to make you confident, and choose to fix your eyes on the One who gives you everything you need. Decide today to carry it out with confidence.

Do you remember what beauty was to you before the world showed you what it says it's supposed to be? Regain your confidence in that, because the world needs more of that. That's why God made you as you are. You are lovely, desirable, chosen, called, purposed, a child of His. And you are deeply loved with great intention.

ONE LAST NOTE

I want to close with this: good times and bad times will both pass, so be intentional with your time. There is no time to waste. Don't wait until you're older and don't wish you were younger. You are who you are, and you are where you are. So thrive in it, babe.

OH, AND ONE MORE THING

This is something I have come to realize about God. If He can stop the waves of the ocean with just one touch, He can stop the waves of my emotions with just one touch as well. He has done that for me time and time again. When you feel overwhelmed, just reach for Him. He will always be there, will always love you, and will never, ever fail you.

This letter is filled with truth from Scripture that you can hold on to. I encourage you to read God's love letter to you and know these truths for yourselves:

- Psalm 139:13
- 1 John 4:18
- Deuteronomy 3:22
- Romans 8:31

- Isaiah 54:17
- Exodus 14:14
- Psalm 91:11
- Genesis 50:20

- Philippians 4:19
- Genesis 1:27
- Psalm 34:10
- Zephaniah 3:17

Live

I'VE WRITTEN SEVERAL BOOKS NOW, AND IF I'VE LEARNED anything about book writing, it's that the deadline always approaches much sooner than I am ready for it. As I sit in my favorite coffee shop with a cinnamon latte today, I realize that with this book, the divine timing of the submission date could not be more amazing.

As I was trying to finish writing very late at night, I got the Instagram itch. Do you know what I am talking about—that urge to post something even though it's midnight? I had recently preached a message I was eager to send out, so I posted it at midnight and went back to writing. I didn't go to bed until 2:25, and when I lay down, I felt the Spirit prompt me to check my Instagram messages, which I know sounds weird—it was weird to me too! I just felt something inside saying to check my messages.

When I clicked on one message, my heart almost stopped. Someone had sent me a message at 1:30 a.m., saying she planned to end her life that night and that she was so hurt because no one knew or seemed to care what she was going to do. She said she was

messaging me because she had just watched my midnight post of me preaching a message on none other than the prodigal son. She felt as though God did not want her and wrote that if she only had someone like me in her life to give her a reason to be alive, it could change things. She finished by wishing me the best in my life and saying she hoped I would go on to do amazing things and thanking me for the video that she got to see before she ended her life.

> God's love is the only love that will remain without failing.

I began to type as fast as I could, hoping I was not too late. I replied to her with a message of love and shared with her that God is not an exclusive God who picks and chooses which of us He loves. I told her He chose her when He gave life to her and that He loved her.

She responded with this: "I am literally sitting on my bedroom floor with a suicide note on one side and a bottle of pills on the other. I told myself that at 2:30 I was going to end it all, and then you messaged me at 2:29."

We continued the conversation, both blown away by God's incredible timing and the fact that she messaged me and that I saw it while writing this book late at night—a book about what it means to truly live. You cannot make this stuff up. She shared with me that she had struggled with anxiety and depression her whole life and that the people who were supposed to love her did a bad job of that. In her words, "I have never really had anyone who has loved me . . . much less the unconditional kind that you talk of. I wouldn't even know where to start."

I did my best to point her down the path of life into the open house of God.

She then thanked me, and her final message was this: "Your response has made me feel much less alone in the world. I still have that part of me that wants to just end it all and stop the pain, but I want to know the feeling that you are talking about. I want to feel the joy that you always exude. I don't want to die, but living is so hard. At times it doesn't feel worth it."

That night, I felt I found my sister in the field with the pigs like the prodigal son I wrote about at the beginning of this book, without any food to fill her stomach. She had reached the point where death seemed to be the only option to end the pain in the place where she was. She did not want to die, but she felt living was not much of an option at that time.

You may feel the same way. Maybe you feel you were on your way to the pigsty alone. You may be with the pigs already, feeling alone, contemplating death, not knowing if there is any reason to be alive, drowning in the loss of hope for love and sense of worth because no house on earth seems to be open to you and no one on earth is welcoming you in. Or maybe you feel like you're living in limbo, going day by day in a sort of half-life that doesn't really feel like living, looking to find life in things that let you down over and over again.

I hope that this book has led you back to life and straight to the perfect love and open arms and open house of God, our Father. That is truly the only place to really live because, as the definition says, to live is "to remain" and "to reside." His love is the only love that will remain without failing, and His home is the only place to reside that you will never lose.

Acknowledgments

THANK YOU, MOM AND DAD, FOR NOT ONLY GIVING ME LIFE but for teaching me how to live. Thank you for an up-close example of what a life with Jesus looks like and for loving me so well. Y'all live to the fullest, and it inspires me.

Thank you to my grandparents and great-grandma for the legacy you have passed down.

Thank you to my team—Stephanie, Courtney, and Morgan—for making every single day of life better. Your lives echo goodness to the world. You all make the world a better place.

Thank you to my soon-to-be husband, Christian, for the life teammate you are. You helped make this book better by sitting with me so many hours and talking things through. I love you.

Thank you to the book team—Beth, Jennifer, and Karissa—for making this book so much better and what it is today.

Notes

1   *About Time*, directed by Richard Curtis, featuring Domhnall Gleeson (Tim Lake), released November 8, 2013, Working Title Films.

2.   Ibid.

3.   Lexico.com, s.v. "live," accessed July 7, 2019, https://www.lexico.com/en/definition/live.

4.   "Suicide Facts," SAVE (Suicide Awareness Voices of Education), accessed November 17, 2019, https://save.org/about-suicide/suicide-facts/.

5.   Dina Spector, "The Odds of You Being Alive Are Incredibly Small," Business Insider, June 11, 2012, https://www.businessinsider.com /infographic-the-odds-of-being-alive-2012-6.

6.   *Cambridge Dictionary*, s.v. "know," accessed October 17, 2019, https://dictionary.cambridge.org/dictionary/english/know.

7.   *Cambridge Dictionary*, s.v. "realize," accessed October 17, 2019, https://dictionary.cambridge.org/dictionary/english/realize.

8.   *Merriam-Webster*, s.v. "fill the gaps," accessed October 17, 2019, https://www.merriam-webster.com/dictionary/fill%20the%20gaps.

9.   TheFreeDictionary.com, s.v. "fill the gap," accessed October 17, 2019, https://idioms.thefreedictionary.com/fill+the+gaps.

10. U.S. Const. amend. I.

11. Chrissy Metz, *This Is Me*, March 27, 2018, HarperAudio, Audible Audiobook.

12. Lexico.com, s.v. "stretch," accessed October 17, 2019, https://www.lexico.com/en/definition/stretch.

13. *The Princess Diaries*, directed by Garry Marshall, featuring Anne Hathaway (Mia Thermopolis) and Heather Matarazzo (Lilly Moscovitz), released July 29, 2001, Walt Disney Pictures.

14. Ibid.

15. *Madagascar*, directed by Eric Darnell and Tom McGrath, released May 27, 2005, DreamWorks Animation.

16. Lexico.com, s.v. "comfort," accessed October 17, 2019, https://www.lexico.com/en/definition/comfort.

17. Lexico.com, s.v. "content," accessed October 17, 2019, https://www.lexico.com/en/definition/content.

18. Will Smith, "What Skydiving Taught Me about Fear," April 26, 2018, YouTube, https://www.youtube.com/watch?v=bFIB05LGtMs.

19. Ibid.

20. *Collins Dictionary*, s.v. "revel," accessed October 17, 2019, https://www.collinsdictionary.com/dictionary/english/revel.

21. *Collins Dictionary*, s.v. "celebrate," accessed October 17, 2019, https://www.collinsdictionary.com/dictionary/english/celebrate.

22. Lexico.com, s.v. "original," accessed October 18, 2019, https://www.lexico.com/en/definition/original.

23. "40 Quotes About Life (for a Pessimist)," *The Telegraph*, updated February 28, 2017, https://www.telegraph.co.uk/books/what-to-read/40-quotes-about-life-for-a-pessimist/jim-carrey-/.

24. Lexico.com, s.v. "like," accessed October 18, 2019, https://www.lexico.com/en/definition/like.

About the Author

S ADIE ROBERTSON, FIRST INTRODUCED TO THE WORLD AS A star of A&E's *Duck Dynasty* and ABC's *Dancing with the Stars*, recognized she could be a positive voice to those in need of an inspiring presence in their lives. At the age of twenty-two, she's become one of the most prominent voices of her generation. Sadie's passion is to speak, to write, to encourage. She is a sister and friend to more than five million followers on her various social platforms, which she sees as a direct line of communication to her peers.

Sadie's creative and entrepreneurial spirit has helped her launch her Live Original brand, which speaks to millions across her various platforms, including YouTube, social media, the *Live Original* blog, LO Fam Community, the Live Original tour, and her *Whoa That's Good* podcast.

Additionally, Robertson has long poured her heart into philan-thropic efforts. She has loved partnering with Roma Boots, Help

One Now, World Vision, and the World Food Program over the last few years. To date, Robertson has been able to be a voice and agent of change in many countries, including Peru, Somalia, Moldova, and the Dominican Republic.

Sadie is newly married to the man of her dreams, Christian, and is looking forward to continuing to learn what it means to truly live and celebrate in every moment of life.